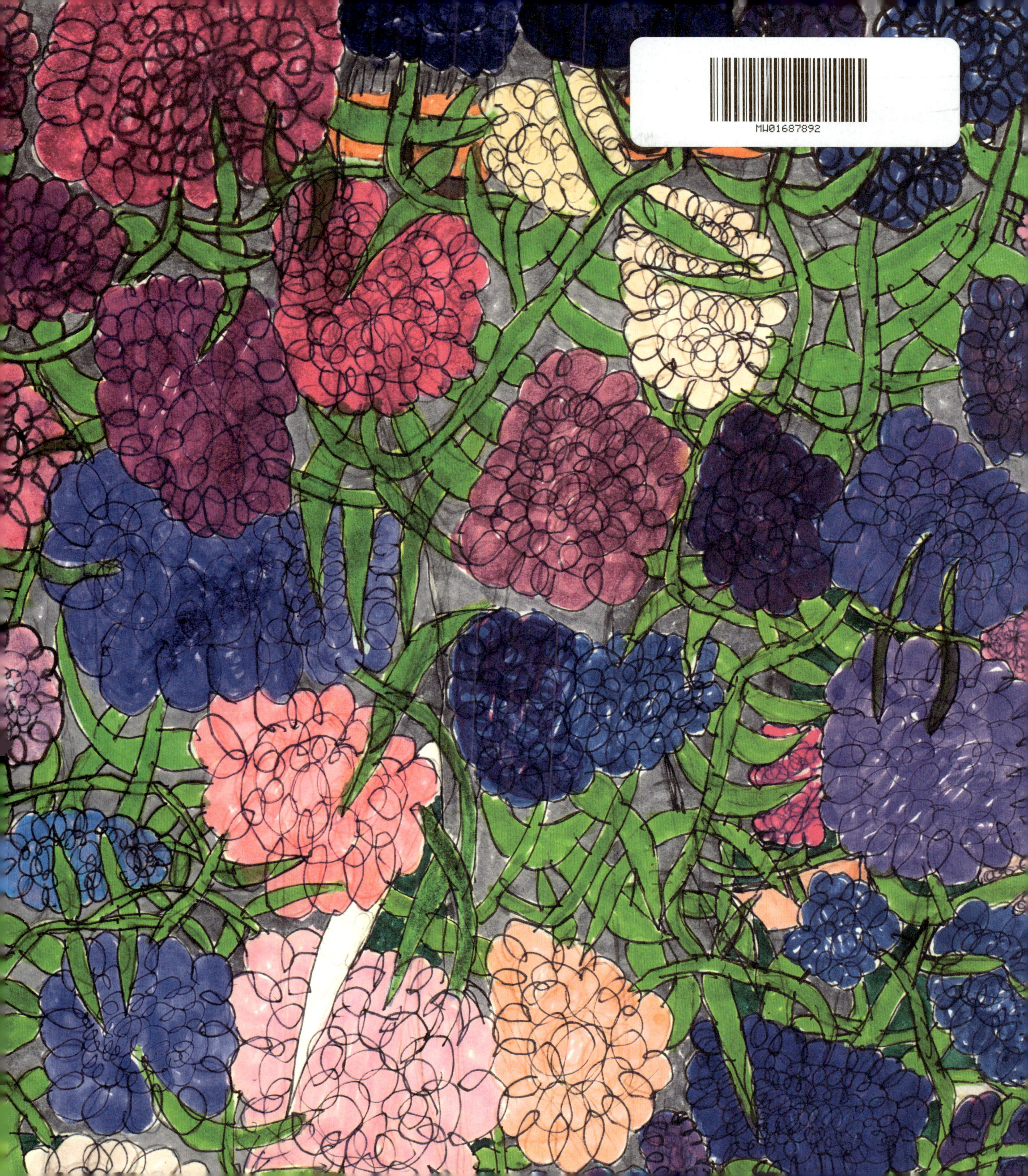

Stuart Williams: His World and His Art

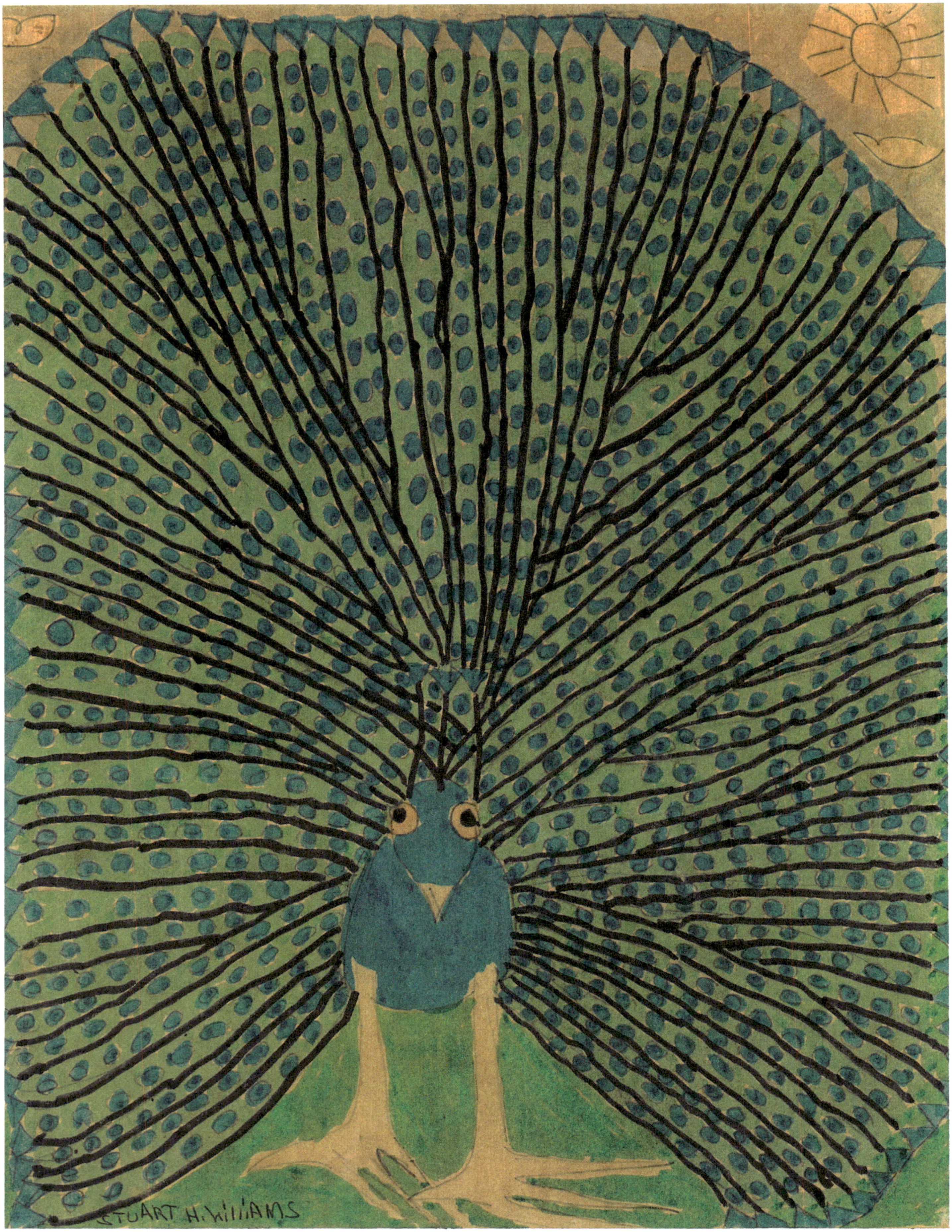
STUART H. WILLIAMS

Stuart Williams: His World and His Art

William Corbett
with an essay by Adrienne Jacobson

Pressed Wafer: Brooklyn

ACKNOWLEDGMENTS

All the Williams brothers and sisters helped in numerous ways. Special thanks to Sydney for his edition of his father's wartime letters and his book on the family; Frank for being behind this book from the start and staying the course; Willard for hosting a reading at the Toadstool Bookshop and directing people who knew Stuart to me; Jenny for coming up with more Stuart art than she knew she had; and Betsy, Charlotte, and George for answering my questions.

And thanks to Joan Doty, Geraldine Hall, Fleur Weymouth, Sharon King, and Larry Hill of Hill Resource Center in Abilene, Texas, Sue Martin, Dr. Sally Eneguess, John Eisenman, Arden Corbett, Nina Nielsen, John Baker, Roy Davis, Cecily Langdale, Abby LaRock, Bill Doreski, Keris Salmon, Paul Doty, Diana Shook, Anne Morris, Julianne Weeks, Rachael Aaruz, and Pressed Wafer's estimable copyeditor Thea Hetzner and proofreader Miles Champion, Michael Russem of Kat Ran Press, and Beverly Corbett.

PRESSED WAFER
375 Parkside Avenue, Brooklyn, NY 11226
www.pressedwafer.com

FRONTISPIECE
Untitled (Peacock)
c. 1990
Marker on cardboard
11 × 14 inches
Collection of Jenny Williams

ISBN 978-1-940396-29-3
FIRST EDITION
Printed in the United States of America

The center of my world was my family, and as a seedling I was lucky to fall on fertile ground.

TOMI UNGERER

Contents

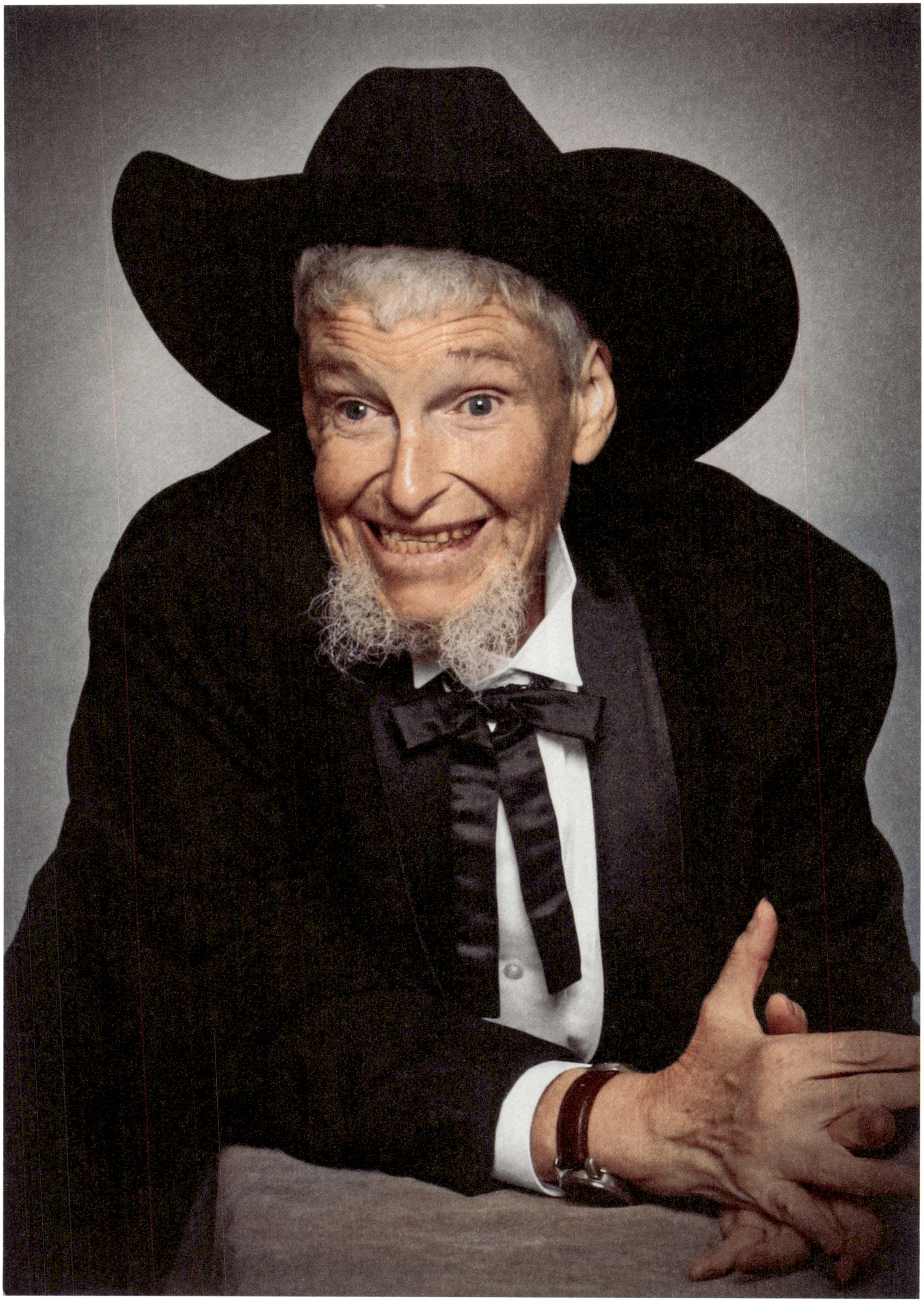

Stuart Williams: His World and His Art

WILLIAM CORBETT

"I wish we were swimming together somewhere without bathing suits in some pool all by itself in some sort of pristine wilderness with soft new grass sprouting all over it, with birds above it and rabbits and such all through it. And the pool should have a willow tree on one side and an oak on the other. The oak should have a large boulder near it, grizzled with lichen and between the boulder and the sun would be ferns and then sweet young grass coming up through the moss, and on the moss we would lie together and the birds would sing and the sun would shine."

Sydney Williams wrote this vision of Eden in a letter to his bride-to-be, Mary Hotchkiss, shortly before they married in 1938. Their son Stuart Williams, the only artist among the nine children born to these two artists, began to paint his own versions of Eden as a teenager. In Stuart's art the birds sing, animals and flowers abound, and the sun always shines. Deer leap in mountain meadows, where juicy grasses taste good. What never appears in Stuart's art are young lovers together on a bed of moss.

Stuart was born in 1950 with the yet-to-be clinically identified Prader–Willi syndrome. This rare, incurable genetic disorder, whose features include the failure to develop sexually, defined Stuart's life but in recompense helped nourish his art. Had he not been a victim of Prader–Willi, Stuart might have grown up to become the dream of his youth, a farmer.

Stuart struggled *not* to be defined by Prader–Willi, but fight though he did, no one can completely overcome such ill luck. His physical limitations caused by weak muscle control, his obsession with food, and, after his mother's death, his frequent attacks of depression—all characteristics of the syndrome—determined much of Stuart's life. But his rich imagination and his ability to express it in art proved a powerful force that opened a world to him when he began to show his work at age sixteen. In an interview he said that when making art he felt his mind to be "frolicking." "I am," Stuart continued, "a very special person inside."

Stuart Williams in 2007 wearing the Western suit he rented for a Willie Nelson concert in Abilene, Texas. He sat in the front row, enjoying himself so thoroughly that Nelson saluted him from the stage.

1 Stuart Hotchkiss Williams had the good fortune to be born to artist parents in Peterborough, New Hampshire, the home of the MacDowell Colony and the model for Thornton Wilder's *Our Town*, a prosperous small town comfortable with art and artists. In 1938 the WPA's *New Hampshire: A Guide to the Granite State* described Peterborough in these words:

> A village of national fame through the MacDowell Colony and Sargent Camp, [Peterborough] lies in a valley of natural beauty formed by the union of the Nubanuit and Contoocook Rivers. Dignified houses line its hilly streets, set against a background of firs and hills, while Grand Monadnock looms behind it in the west. A combination of industries and summer activities, Peterborough hears on one side the whir of textile looms and on the other the music of Edward MacDowell. This gives the village an air of being larger than it really is and the fine modern buildings, mostly of brick and having a Georgian simplicity, add to the impression.

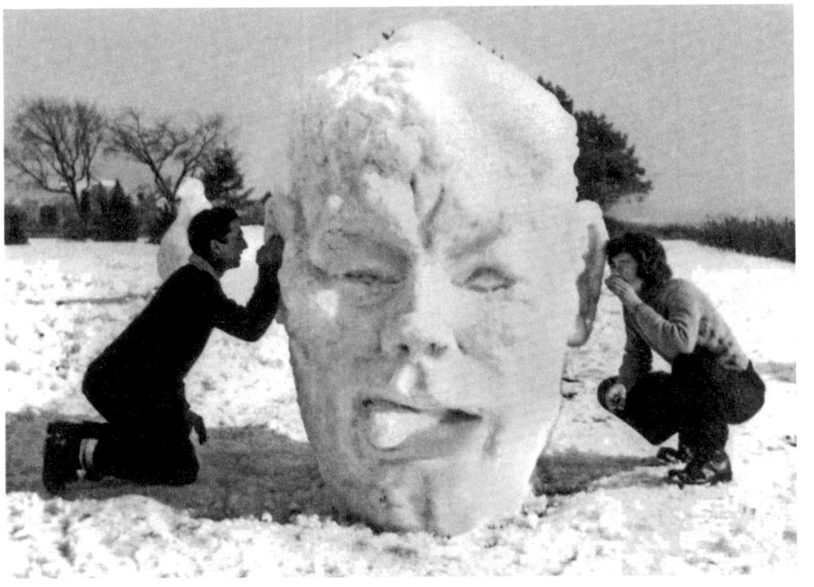

Sydney and Mary talking through a snowman's head.

> The summer colonies, devoted chiefly to artistic expression, have brought to Peterborough an intellectual background usually found only in college towns.

Peterborough's intellectual and artistic climate would provide Stuart with venues for his art unavailable in all but a very few other New England towns of its size.

Sydney Williams and Mary Hotchkiss were born into wealthy families in Wellesley, Massachusetts, and New Haven, Connecticut, respectively. They were reared in great houses staffed by servants. Children of privilege, both developed independent streaks that would shape their life together. After graduating from Harvard, Sydney was determined to become a sculptor. Mary graduated from Virginia's Foxcroft School, to which she had brought her horse, and then studied art in Italy and at Yale Art School, which she did not like and left after a year. She went to Boston to study under the sculptor George Demetrios at the School of the Museum of Fine Arts, where Sydney was also a student. He concentrated on the figure, and Mary on horses.

After a big wedding—a matron of honor and five bridesmaids attended Mary, and Sydney had a best man and nine ushers—they honeymooned in northwestern Connecticut before making their home in Peterborough in the summer of 1938. Sydney's family had long summered there, and the newlyweds moved into the Dodge Place, an unwinterized farmhouse without electricity owned by Sydney's parents. They had a view of the mountains, the area's predominant geographical feature. This would be the Williamses' home until Mary's death, in 1990. The house still stands on a hillside of hardscrabble land, but trees now obscure the view.

Sydney and Mary had three children, Mary, Sydney Jr., and Frank, in quick succession. In the early years they made for their family a simple, rustic farm-style life. They heated their home with the wood that Sydney logged and carried home on a horse-drawn sleigh or carriage, depending on the season. They kept animals, most significantly the horses that would be a center of family life. In the 1960s Sydney and Mary might have been considered back-to-the-land hippies. They were, in the words of their daughter Betsy, "just plain different." Supported by small trusts, they lived modestly but not in rebellion against their families. They were unconventional yet retained at least some of the rituals of their class. Three daughters were given coming-out parties in Mary's Connecticut hometown. During many summers the family spent weeks at Mary's family summer home on the Connecticut shore. They always brought along the family pony and sometimes a few goats.

Although neighbors and friends describe the Williams house as like a farmhouse (meaning the emphasis was not on housecleaning but on the outdoors), the family did not farm. Their part of New Hampshire is hilly, rocky, and threaded with rivers, streams, ponds, and lakes—unfit for farming but just right for the mills that once hummed and now stand empty. In addition to horses, they kept ducks, peacocks, barn cats and dogs, and the goats that provided the family's milk.

In 1944, Sydney, a passionate lifelong skier, went off to war, serving with the 10th Mountain Division in

The Williams family, summer 1950. Front row, from left: Sydney Jr., with a platter of Red Shed toy animals; Frank, with the bust his father made of him; Betsy; Mary, holding Jenny; and Charlotte. Back row: Mary, holding baby Stuart, and Sydney.

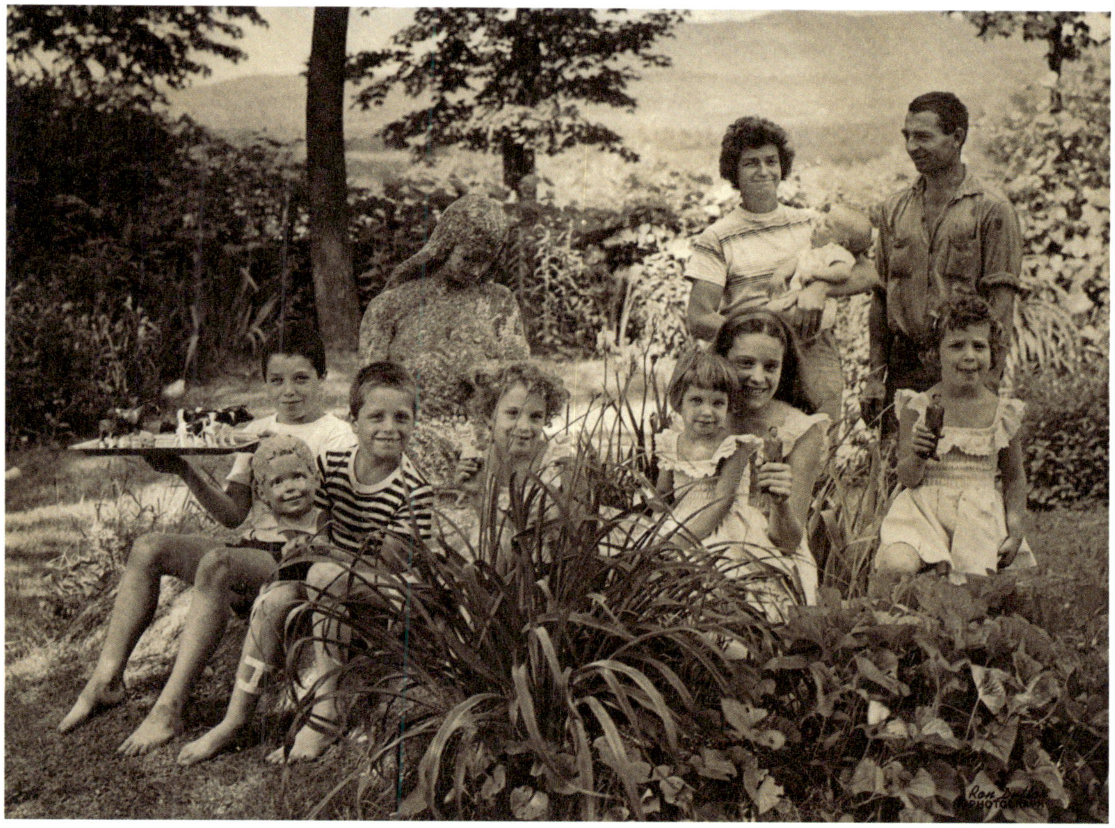

Italy. Upon his return, the couple had three daughters, Betsy, Charlotte, and Jenny, before Stuart arrived in 1950. Two more sons, Willard and George, completed the family.

The Williams children were reared in a home without television but with a fertile disorder of books and art-making equipment. They did not have their own rooms but improvised, moving around the house as they grew. Some visitors remember the home as "full of stuff" and "chaos." How could it have been otherwise with a brood of children in and out all day, free to pick up a book or sit down to draw wherever paper and pencils were handy?

When Stuart was born, Prader–Willi syndrome was six years away from being described. Because one characteristic evident at birth is low muscle tone, Stuart's symptoms would likely have been classed under the umbrella term "floppy child disease." Mary, who had nursed six children, most probably was quick to notice the difficulty Stuart had with feeding. His brother Sydney recalls that their parents and the doctors knew at birth that something was not right with Stuart, and that blood tests had also suggested some sort of problem. In Sydney's words, "the prognosis was that he might live to twenty, perhaps thirty years."

We cannot be sure exactly when Mary and Sydney knew for certain that Stuart was not like their other children. The older children remember that the family accepted Stuart as different, with some accommodations being made for his slow physical development, but he was not, for the most part, treated as exceptional. The family did not concentrate on Stuart's future but on his day-to-day present. Years later, sometime in the early 1970s, daughter Mary chanced upon a newspaper article on Prader–Willi, and the family gained a name for and a more detailed understanding of Stuart's condition.

His father, who stubbornly insisted that Stuart keep up with his siblings in physical activities, made a decision that would determine Stuart's life for years to come. Recognizing that because of poor muscle tone Stuart's hands were weak and clumsy, making it difficult for him to perform simple tasks, Sydney put Stuart in charge of the family's small herd of Toggenburg goats. Beyond developing a sense of responsibility, Sydney hoped that milking the goats might strengthen the boy's fingers and hands. Stuart became a goat keeper at around age six and remained one into his mid-forties. His hands became, in the words of his sister Betsy, "incredibly strong." As did, to his misfortune, his thirst for goat milk. His father also tried to make Stuart into a hiker, skier, and equestrian like his brothers and sisters, demands that he could not meet and came to resent. In putting him in charge of the goats, Sydney gave Stuart a task at which he could succeed; in time, goats became a core subject of his art.

At the age of twenty-four, Stuart wrote in an autobiographical note for his 1976 color calendar, "When I was six years old, I got started in my art from watching other people draw." Those other people were his parents and some, if not all, of his brothers and sisters. Stuart's surviving family remember that he drew constantly, producing cards for everyone's birthdays and at Christmas. No one had to encourage him; the Williams family left Stuart alone to do what he enjoyed doing.

When he turned six Stuart entered Miss Linderman's Gosling School, a Peterborough grade school he attended until the age of twenty. There he was treated as exceptional only in that Miss Linderman allowed him to stay until he had outgrown the school. Stuart learned his numbers, and to read—the beginning of a lifelong devotion to books—and to write. He had the good fortune of being left alone to draw as he pleased. It seems that no teacher tried to bend Stuart to a standard. Early on, one of his teachers noted in an evaluation, "He is outstanding in drawing—a gifted, specially endowed individual."

Miss Linderman's allowed Stuart to develop in his own way, at his own pace, while encouraging him to participate in the life of the school. He appeared as a caroler in school Christmas programs and acted in plays, including *Puck of Pook's Hill.* Surviving school records, most of them undated and all unsigned, on file at the Peterborough Historical Society provide this portrait of Stuart as a student:

"Stuart Williams has had insights into his arithmetic he has never had before. He likes to write stories and they always contribute to the class. He has opinions to offer in discussions and is seeing relationships, as he never has before. Above all he is being a boy among boys."

"He sees relations in original ways."

"Stuart has a creative approach to his studies. He wants to push through to understanding. This year he has particularly enjoyed economics, which he prepares on his own initiative. His drawing develops each year and should be an avocation in his lifetime, at least I say 'avocation' because Stuart insists he is going to be a farmer."

"He is seeing the study of wild animals as a new body of knowledge to augment with further pursuits possibly in connection with field observations."

"He has a genuine interest in economics. His love for reading and writing stories, his unfailing courtesy—an interesting person in his own right."

Miss Linderman's reflects Peterborough's progressive character. Had Stuart been reared in a different town, who knows what his luck might have been? Had the only option for his family been a public school, it is doubtful that he would have enjoyed the freedom and been given the care afforded by Miss Linderman's.

But there was also a dark side to Stuart's Gosling School days. His obvious handicaps made him a target for boys who tormented and bullied him. Many years

Stuart gave this painting to his art teacher Bea Orchard. Made sometime in his early teens, it is the earliest painting by Stuart on record.

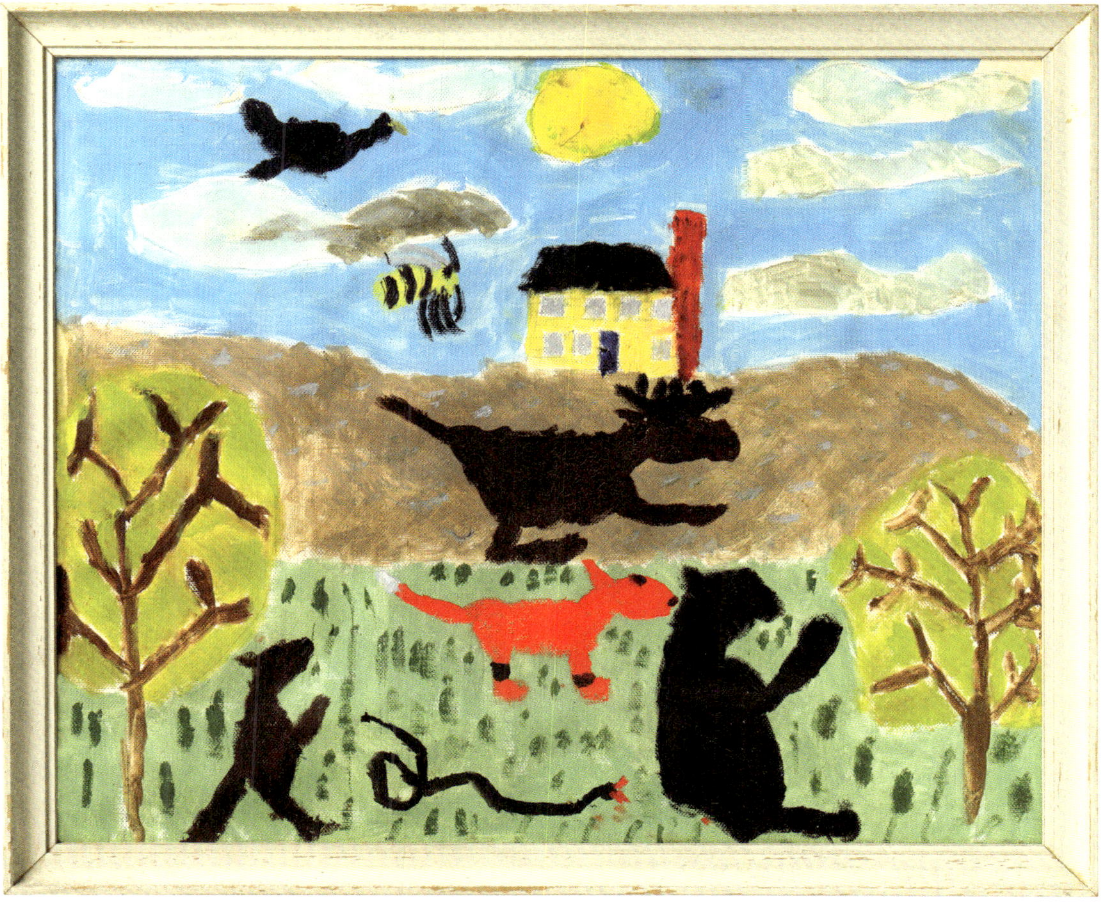

later he revealed that two particularly nasty boys had sexually molested him. For all its civic virtue, Peterborough could not escape common human cruelty.

When Stuart was thirteen, his mother took him to art classes at the Sharon Arts Center in nearby Sharon, New Hampshire. There he encountered the artist and teacher Fleur Weymouth and learned a decisive lesson.

In "They're Gonna Make Me Draw Themselves," her essay on teaching art to children, Weymouth noted, "I'm not against accuracy in art, but not at the expense of what is living and probably lopsided. We all know *life* when we see it." Weymouth brought this spirit to her work with Stuart in the two years he took classes at Sharon. He had another teacher there, painter Bea Orchard, whom he liked enough to give an oil painting to, but Weymouth imparted the lesson that would sustain him throughout his working life.

This occurred at their first meeting. Weymouth recounts:

> Mary brought him to my children's art class at the Sharon Arts Center. He was unable to get his winter parka on and off by himself. He was thirteen; he couldn't fit all the goats and peacocks on their farm onto one page, and he was upset. I do remember the *moment* when I spread the fingers of my left hand out over the blank paper in front of Stuart and then spread the fingers of my right hand over them at about a 45 degree angle, to show him that not only could he fit all his goats and peacocks onto one page by placing one hand in front of another, so that just parts showed, but that he could put anything else in as well.
>
> A smile the size of a river opened up on his face (he'd been drawing everything side by side). The same day I brought a book of Henri Rousseau jungle paintings for him to look at.
>
> Like most little boys, he disliked sloppy watercolors, where things ran into one another. He preferred things separate and clean. He loved pencils, and later on his family gave him color ink pens.
>
> His talent was evident from the word go.

It is impossible to say how quickly Weymouth's lesson liberated and focused Stuart's imagination.

Those with Prader-Willi usually have trouble learning new things, but once a thing is learned, it's rarely if ever forgotten. Stuart's memory was so prodigious that Mary came to call him her "computer." During early interviews for this book, if his siblings could not answer a question, they all said, "Stuart will know." Two months before his death, I interviewed Stuart at the Hill Resource Center in Abilene, Texas, where he lived. Although he did not, as I had been warned, make conversation, his answers to my questions were terse and precise; then he waited patiently for the next question. His memory appeared to be excellent.

Weymouth bought examples of Stuart's early work and photographed some of the work he did with markers, knowing that the colors would fade. She actively championed his art, enlisting him and the photographers Esther Titcomb and George Weymouth in two shows in Peterborough during the summer of 1974. "Stuart outsold us all," she recalls. A few years later she shared printing costs for the first postcard reproductions of Stuart's work.

After moving to Captiva Island in Florida in the 1980s, Weymouth befriended the artist Robert Rauschenberg. Showing him around her house, she directed his attention to a work by Stuart and asked what he thought. "Oh," Rauschenberg exclaimed, "a genius!"

In 1966 the Monadnock Music Festival inaugurated its annual Christmas Fair. Stuart exhibited his work, a natural step for him to take, and would continue to show there on and off through the 1980s. Bonnie Siegel, who produced the fair, remembers that Stuart bought a sales booth for several years and took intense pleasure in selling his work and chatting with buyers. Stuart always enjoyed meeting those interested in his art and relished talking about his pictures.

On December 2, 1968, Stuart's eighteenth birthday, Sydney Williams died of lung cancer. Stuart would be haunted by this event, an anxious dread that mounted and deepened with the deaths of other family members on his birthday decades later. He came to blame himself for his father's death and those that followed.

Stuart had resented his father for forcing him to go on family hikes and ski trips, activities that he could barely perform. Though his father had urged him to go beyond his limits, he also taught Stuart about plants, a lifelong knowledge that emerged clearly in his art, and encouraged his art-making. Sydney Jr. has described their father as a "gentle and empathetic man . . . a nonconformist in the mold of Henry David Thoreau—he loved his family, his independence and his art." Some of these qualities lived on in Stuart.

At the time of their father's death, Stuart's older siblings had moved out of the Dodge Place. Only Stuart, Willard, and the youngest Williams child, George, were left there with Mary. At some point, Mary began to notice that food was disappearing. In order to protect Stuart from his insatiable hunger, she padlocked the refrigerator and kitchen cupboards. Over the twenty-two years they lived together, Mary's efforts met with mixed success, and Stuart came to resent her, as he would all caregivers who controlled his diet. His uncontrollable obsession with food could be thwarted, but it never went away, and the wily Stuart often responded to restrictions in his home by eating the grain he fed his goats and drinking their milk. George recalls that Stuart had an uncanny ability to pick locks and was

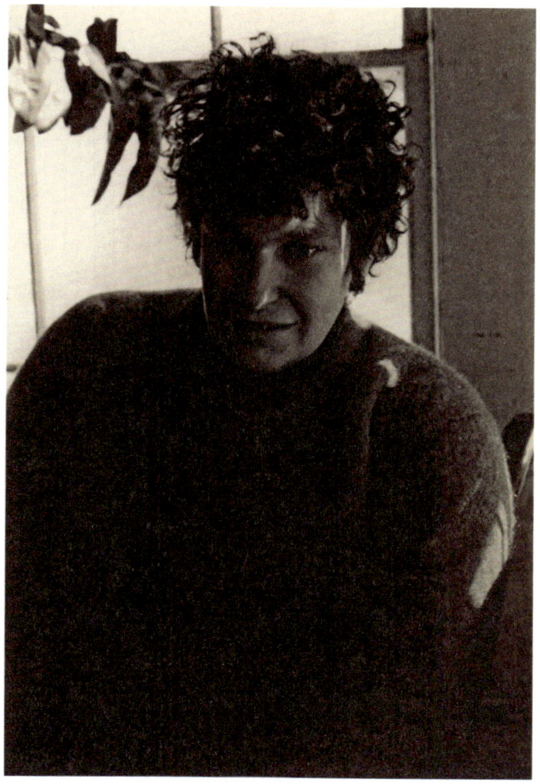

Stuart at twenty.

clever enough to unscrew hinges to get to the food forbidden to him.

By now Stuart was very troubled by how different he was from his siblings and his peers. His father had done all he could to make sure that Stuart dressed and behaved like the other children. But Mary, alone, could not keep him to this standard. Their constant arguments and struggles over food reflected Stuart's deeper frustration at being afflicted with Prader–Willi. He had grown into adult rages and depression.

Since 1966, Stuart had made calendars for the family. In 1970, the year he finished his fourteenth and last year at the Gosling School, he published his 1971 calendar in black and white and offered it for sale at the Monadnock Music Christmas Fair on the advice of a friend. This calendar introduces Stuart as a writer. Along with a brief autobiographical sketch—"I live on a farm with six goats, eight horses, twelve chickens, one rabbit and one beautiful peacock."—he provided captions for every month.

Prader–Willi typically causes malformation of the feet. As a boy this made it difficult for Stuart to keep up with his athletic family, and the condition worsened over time, necessitating special boots and leg braces. In the 1970s Stuart had to go to Boston for these and wore them throughout the rest his life. Still, he more shambled than walked.

In 1971 his sister Jenny, two years older than Stuart and his closest friend among his siblings, took him on a trip to Switzerland to see the homeland of his beloved Toggenburg goats. She has explained that since Stuart, limited in movement and stamina, "never got to do anything," she wanted to get him out of his rut. On the trip he slept a lot, lost weight, and drew constantly with his markers. The Swiss mountain houses set atop barns were a favorite subject.

On his return Stuart concentrated on drawing goats. His goats are cartoony, goofily so. His interest was always less in anatomical correctness than in what his goats meant to him, his feeling for them as characters. Those who saw Stuart with his goats remember how they ran to him, how he spoke to them and moved slowly among them, stroking them. He was confident in his mastery and stewardship of his herd. Against significant odds he managed to maintain a small herd until 1996.

Stuart's first color calendar appeared in 1972, the year Jenny and younger brother Willard founded the Toadstool Bookshop in Peterborough. From the start they displayed Stuart's work and sold his postcards and calendars. That same year he completed his most ambitious work to date, a six-foot-wide, eight-foot-high mural for his friend Jim Haddock's Monadnock Family Services office in Keene, New Hampshire. In 1992 the mural was moved to the Monadnock Children's Museum, which closed in 1998 without, it seems, finding a home for Stuart's work. The mural has since disappeared.

Stuart did not publish a calendar for 1973, but in 1974 a color calendar with a peacock on the cover appeared. In his "About the Artist by the Artist" statement, he wrote:

> This fall, the last weekend in October, I am planning to have a one man show of my work in my studio, which is a little way down the road from the farm.

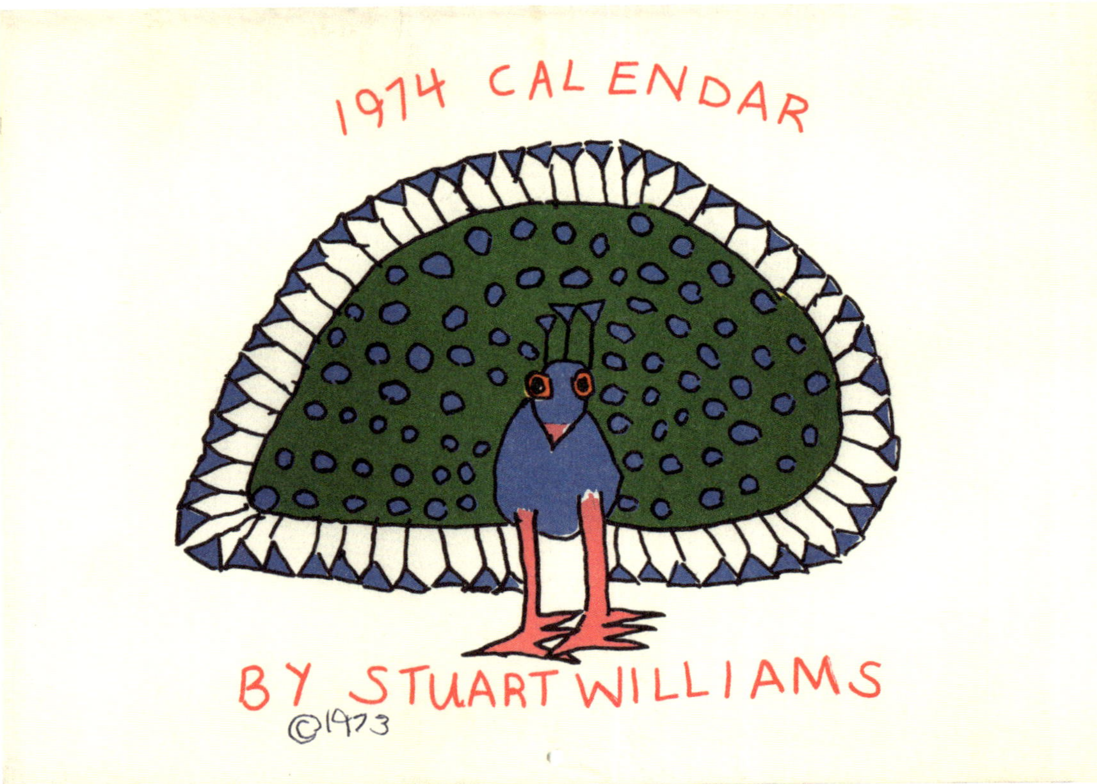

In his 1974 calendar, Stuart's note "About The Artist By The Artist" reads in part: "My main interests in art have been my calendars and my oil paintings, some of which I have done for commissions. '71 was the year I had my first calendar printed in black and white. For '72, the first colored one was printed. The main reason we skipped '73 was my mother said there wasn't enough time." Calendars could be ordered directly from Stuart.

This year I started doing posters. The first one I did was started at the Craftsman's Fair in Sunapee, and I didn't finish it until this winter. The poster is of wild and tame animals. Last year I used my room to do oil painting in my spare time. This year I have my own studio, which is a great help. I am really getting underway, and I can keep more than one project going at once. The main reason why I am starting to use the studio is that my family complained about the poster getting in the way. Now I am working on a Noah's Ark scene, which is also a poster.

The demands of a one-man show in nearby Hancock's library caused Stuart to skip a 1975 calendar. But late that year he produced his 1976 "Noah's Ark" calendar, his last and most beautifully printed calendar, complete with a statement in which he wrote, "My main interests in art have been my calendars and my oil paintings, and my posters which I have done in magic markers. Some of which I have done for commissions."

In 1975 the Iselin family opened the Folkways Café on Grove Street in downtown Peterborough. This became the center for an active local music scene and a stop for touring performers. From the start Widdy Iselin and her family championed Stuart's work, giving him shows and putting new pictures on display. Many remember first seeing Stuart's work hung on the Folkways' walls. By this point the twenty-five-year-old Stuart had shown his work in a number of venues, and some of that work had sold. Stuart kept no record of sales or even an archive of his pictures, however, and we have no idea of what he showed where, what he sold to whom, or for how much.

Stuart, like his family and most who bought his art, took his work for granted at least for the first decades of his career. Making art was his constant preoccupation, so constant that his birthday and Christmas cards, while saved (many are still extant), were thought of not as fine art to be framed or otherwise preserved but just as something that Stuart did. When each of his brothers and sisters married, he made wedding pictures for them—always received as meaningful gifts but not treasured as works of art. Many of these exist today, but few are in excellent shape. Unless treated with great care, his Magic Marker colors quickly faded. His early work went not to collectors but to family and friends, few of whom were aware that such care was necessary.

Stuart left no record that this relative neglect mattered to him. At work here may have been Stuart's near total indifference to art other than his own. Since

Stuart in Egypt on his first trip to Africa. Photograph by Jenny Williams.

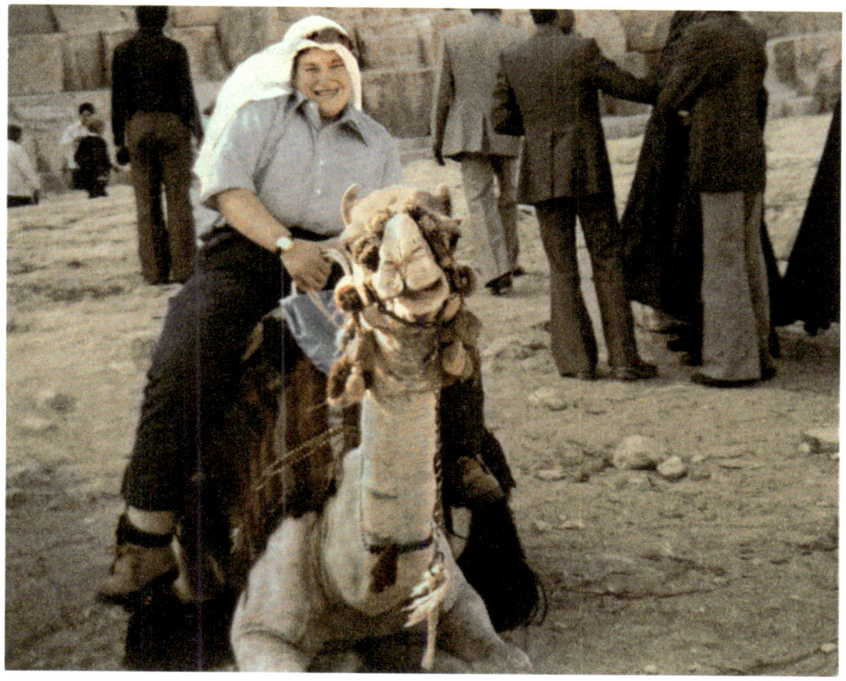

he did not visit galleries or museums, he probably did not consider his art as deserving the respect shown in those places. There is little sign that he thought of himself as having a conventional career in the art world or building a body of work. He appears to have made art for the simplest of reasons: the act of making pictures gave him pleasure. And it gave him pleasure as well to sell or give away what he made.

Thanks to Geraldine Hall we have a portrait of Stuart and his mother in 1976. Willard had married and moved from the Dodge Place, and George lived across the road in a cottage called the "Love-nest." The ten-year-old Hall had been sent to take riding lessons from Mary on the advice that "if you really want to ride and appreciate horses, Mary Williams is the one to teach you." Hall quickly came to adore Mary as much for her interest in a ten-year-old as for her command of horses. Mary liked Hall, hiring her to muck out the stables and work around the barn. She began to ride her bicycle across Peterborough to the Dodge Place as often as she could. She remembers the Williams house as "magical, full of art and all the animals."

On first meeting Stuart, Hall says, "I wasn't sure if he was a man or a boy, partly because he was so quiet and the men I knew were not quiet at all." Stuart befriended her, and she helped him care for his goats, hard work for someone her age. His goats were a constant topic in the household, especially when the kids were born. A goatherd can have only so many male kids, which meant a number had to be given away. Stuart struggled with this every year.

Hall recalls Stuart as "very stubborn" but kind and funny. She remembers the chain across the family refrigerator, and Mary and Stuart squabbling over his desire to get a television. He wanted to watch nature shows; Mary refused to break the family rule for him.

As he did with so many friends, Stuart generously gave Hall artworks, paintings she carried with her through many moves over nearly forty years. It was not until the last time she saw Stuart, however—at the Williams family exhibition in 1990—that she first realized that he was not just someone who made pictures but an artist in his own right.

In 1977, Jenny took Stuart on another trip, this time to Africa: Egypt for a week and then Tanzania and Kenya. The animals Stuart saw in Kenya had a profound effect on his art, and he would return to the giraffes, lions, elephants, and antelopes he had seen there into the 1990s.

Long a passionate reader, after visiting Africa, Stuart read more widely on animals, especially gorillas, and on natural history in general. After his mother's death, he was able to expand his interest through television nature programs and ultimately collected a library of DVDs.

At some point in the early 1980s, Robert "Mac" Doty, director of Manchester, New Hampshire's Currier Museum of Art, the state's foremost public museum, chanced to see a poster by Stuart. (A family story has it that Doty first saw Stuart's work when he called at the Dodge Place to look at a horse. Since Doty did ride and kept a horse throughout his years at the Currier, he may well have visited the Williamses' farm for that purpose, but in interviews Doty mentioned the poster.) He was impressed enough to pursue Stuart, and this led to a solo exhibition at the Currier, the show that lifted Stuart out of small-town arts and crafts venues.

It was great good fortune for Stuart that Mac Doty saw that poster, for Doty was an exceptional curator with a wide range of interests. The Boston gallery owner Nina Nielsen has remarked, "Doty didn't come from a little world and was not going to stay in one." He began his curatorial career at the George Eastman House in Rochester, New York. His first book was on the Photo-Secession group. From the Eastman House he went to the Albright-Knox Art Gallery in Buffalo, New York, where he became friends with the curator Gordon Smith. Doty next joined Governor Nelson Rockefeller's Empire State Plaza project in Albany, New York. This sent him around the country to visit all sorts of art venues as well as artists' studios. Doty then went to Manhattan's Whitney Museum of American Art, where he again roved the country, putting his eclectic eye to work in service of the Whitney Biennial. At the Whitney he curated a number of shows, including a major survey of American photographs, *Photography in America*, the exhibitions *Human Concern/Personal Torment: The Grotesque in American Art* (1969) and *Contemporary Black Artists in America* (1971), and shows of work by Lucas Samaras and Adolph Gottlieb.

In *Human Concern/Personal Torment*, Doty caught the Vietnam era, a most grotesque American political and social moment. The specificity and breadth of the art he selected went beyond commentary, opening out into a view of the American imagination. He hung Willem de Kooning's *Woman and Bicycle* next to David Smith's *Medals for Dishonor* and works by Thomas Nast, George Bellows, and R. Crumb, as well as Peter Saul, Bruce Conner, Paul Thek, Edward Kienholz, and Jim Nutt that more than forty years later keep their edge.

After the Whitney, Doty became the director of the Akron Art Institute in Ohio. He left there for the Currier, drawn by Gordon Smith's recommendation of the institution as well as its small but choice collection and the freedom that the gallery offered him—even making available a small space in which he could show whatever he wanted. Doty's first-rate eye was keen for folk art and antiques, as well as painters as diverse as Will Barnet, Al Held, and Neil Welliver, all of whom he gave shows at the Currier.

The poster that set Doty in search of Stuart is unknown. Doty's notes on Stuart's Currier exhibition are few—it was not his habit to document shows in detail. It *was* his habit to work closely with his artists, but the Williams family has scant recollection of Doty and remembers no family involvement in the show. When *The World of Stuart Williams* opened on November 25, 1986, according to his older brother Frank, "It blew us away. Everyone was absolutely thrilled."

There were twenty-two works in the show, dating from 1984, *Beware Bear*, to 1986. The majority—seventeen—were from 1986, when Stuart had again traveled

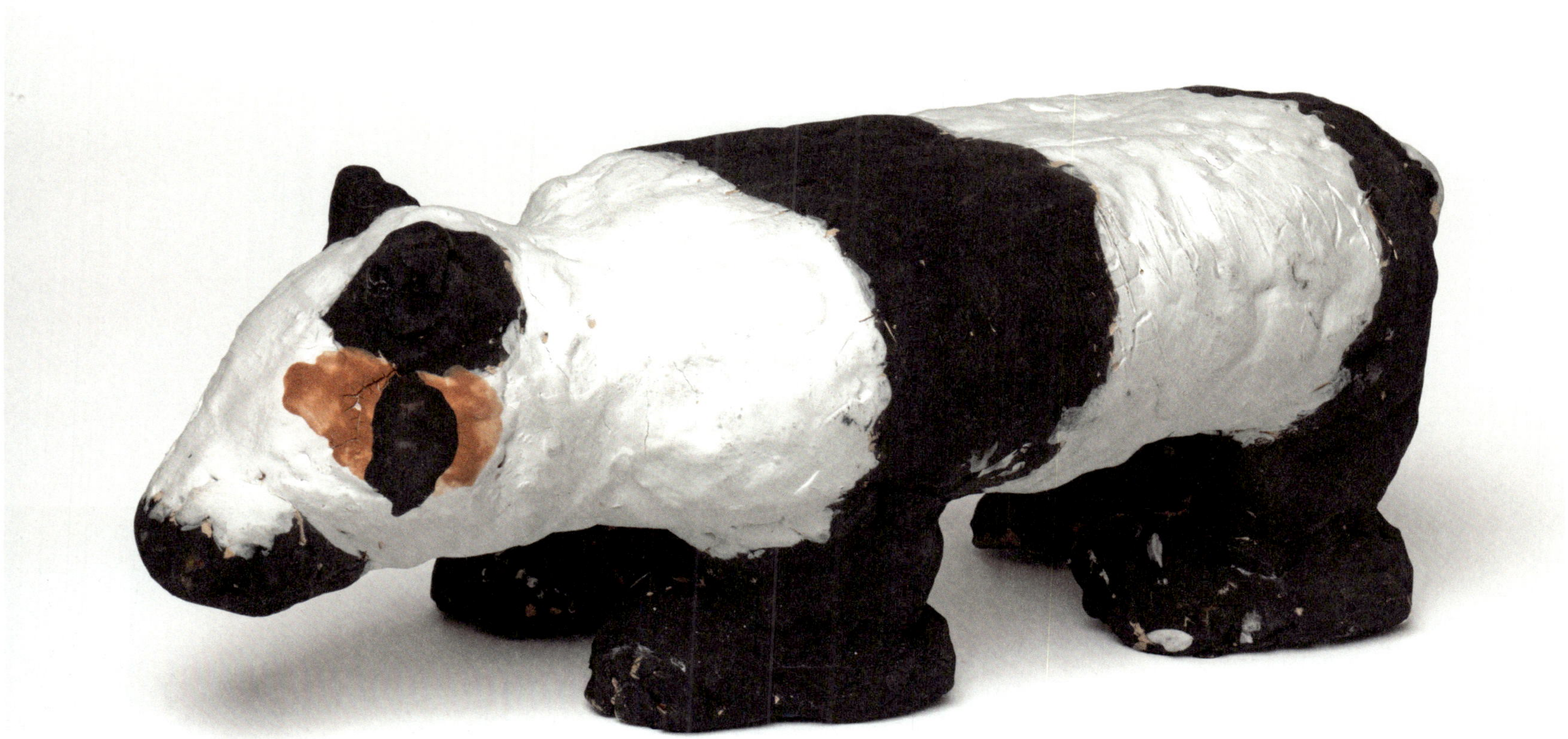

Panda, acrylic on clay, n.d. Stuart made few sculptures. This one probably dates from his time in Abilene.

to Africa, this time in the company of his nineteen-year-old niece, Mary's daughter, Robina. They spent three weeks touring wildlife parks in Kenya and traveling to the Serengeti plains in Tanzania. They saw elephants, giraffes, lions, antelope, wildebeests, hyenas, and many different birds, including large flocks of flamingos at Lake Naivasha. Most evenings Stuart sketched the animals they had seen that day. Robina recounts that "Stuart collected carved wooden animals and bought at least ten while we were there."

Stuart's Currier show sold out. Doty himself bought *Beware Bear* and *Dressage Champion!* No record of other buyers has come to light.

Doty's interest in Stuart's work did not end with the Currier show. He put Stuart's *Squirrel and Bird* in the Currier's 1989 *By Good Hands: New Hampshire Folk Art*. When Doty curated the *Recent American Folk Art Exhibition* for Manchester, New Hampshire's Hatfield Gallery, a drawing by Stuart of two elephants appeared on the announcement card. At New England College's Hancock Gallery, his last curatorial position, Doty again gave Stuart a show. Before Mac Doty, Stuart had enjoyed no association with the larger art world, and it is unlikely that Stuart or anyone on his behalf would have approached the Currier. It was pure luck that the eye of this gifted curator happened upon Stuart's art.

Throughout the 1980s, Stuart's obsession with food intensified. Since Mary held the keys to the food supply, she became the target of Stuart's rage when he could not gain access to the food his insatiable appetite demanded. In the late 1980s, he began to gain weight steadily. When he fed his goats, he sometimes ate their grain and drank their milk. He may have had other sources of food as well. On a May morning in 1987, Mary found him in his room barely able to breathe. Dr. Sally Eneguess admitted Stuart to Monadnock Regional Hospital with a diagnosis of respiratory failure and associated morbid obesity, the cause of death for many Prader-Willi sufferers. She did not expect him to survive.

Monadnock Regional held demons for Stuart that tormented him during the early days of his hospitalization. His father had died there, and Stuart refused to be put into any of the rooms he remembered. Although Dr. Eneguess was unable to find him a room in another area facility, gradually Stuart calmed down; after a tracheotomy he began a slow recovery, losing weight as his condition improved over the nearly three weeks he spent in the hospital.

After returning home, even though he was too weak to look after his goats, Stuart continued to lose weight. When he had shed a hundred pounds, the family gave him a party to celebrate his weight loss and encourage his self-discipline. At the party Dr. Eneguess spoke of how near death he had been and of her fears for him. To mark the occasion, the family gave Stuart two fifty-pound bags of grain for his goats, each one more than he could lift, a reminder of how harmful regaining the weight would be.

Dr. Eneguess became Stuart's friend—she remembers that his likes and dislikes were clear and emphatic, and he liked her—and looked after him for the next four years, until she left Peterborough. She witnessed the profound and pervasive effects Prader-Willi inflicted on his everyday life, recalling that Stuart did not want to eat in front of people. Once she observed him as he ate half a grapefruit in "no apparent order, like an animal"; twenty-five years later, this memory of Stuart's feeding ferocity still disquieted her. His sister Jenny remembers that during childhood Stuart's table manners were proper, but "when grown up, he was aware that his hunger drove him to eat in a somewhat uncivilized way, and it probably made him prefer not to be seen." This need had to add yet another complication to Stuart's obsession with food.

During her time with Stuart, Dr. Eneguess gathered that over the months when his weight spiked he had not been making art. This may explain why he gave her an unfinished oil painting from that period. It hung on her kitchen wall for years until it was replaced by one of her daughter's paintings. In hospital and during his recovery, he did not, so far as she remembers, draw, but he often spoke about his hopes that people could be, *needed* to be, educated about Prader-Willi. When she chanced to see Stuart over the years before he moved to Abilene, he was always funny and winning, a near universal description given by those who saw Stuart infrequently. He had a "street angel" charm.

In 1988, Abby La Rock, an occupational therapist living down Middle Hancock Road from the Williams farm, got to know Mary and Stuart. She and her daughter Leah went to Mary for riding lessons, and they boarded their horses in the Williamses' barn. La Rock was at the farm almost every day to care for her horses. She grew close to Mary and Stuart and remembers Stuart as "always talkative... a good friend." When he wasn't working in the two light-filled rooms converted for him from his father's studio, he drew outside with wax crayons. Like all those I've spoken to who saw Stuart at his home, La Rock remembers his goats. Stuart had become a devotee of country music, an enthusiasm he retained until the end of his life; she recounts his naming a Billy goat George Jones and two does Dolly Parton and Loretta Lynn.

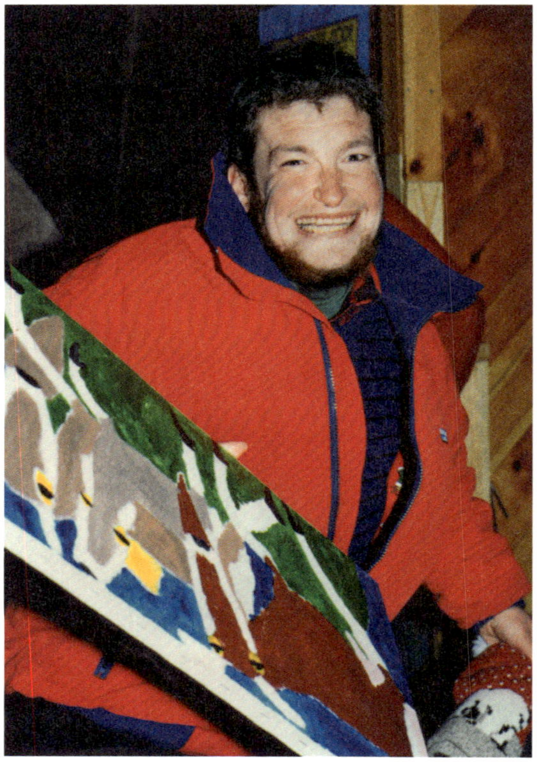

Stuart in 1988, arriving at the Monadnock Music Christmas Fair.

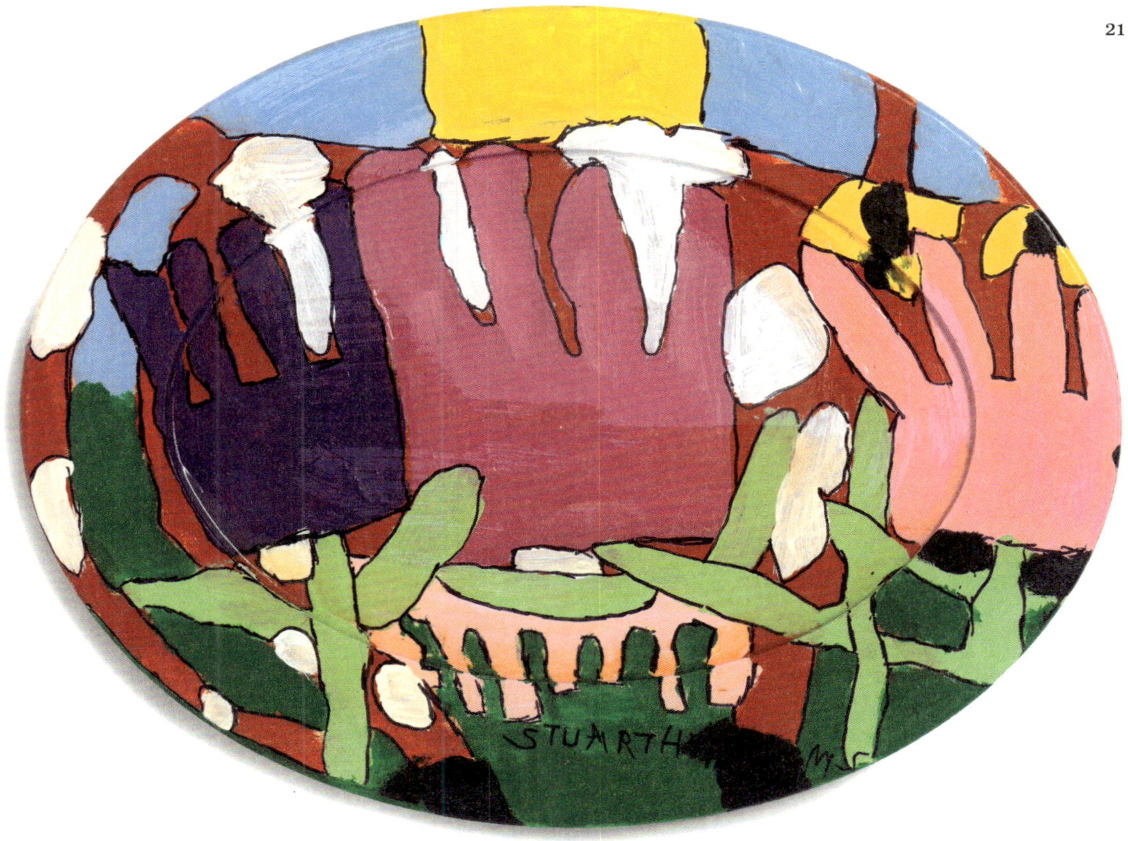

Serving tray, acrylic on wood.

La Rock's professional experience and training gave her a special, unique insight into Stuart and Mary's life together. In the parlance of her trade, she speaks of Stuart at his drawing and caring for his goats as moving "rotely for what he did": his motions were mechanical, learned behaviors that did not come naturally to him.

La Rock describes Mary with obvious admiration, both for her as a person and for her intuitive grasp of Stuart's condition and her attentive, patient manner with him. She remembers Mary and Stuart in their tattered "snowflake" sweaters—the Dodge Place now had oil heat but was draughty—over convivial cups of tea. They drank Red Rose for the porcelain animals that came in each box, groups of which were scattered around the living room. As with other friends, Stuart was generous to La Rock, giving her cards on her birthday and several pictures.

On November 30, 1990, the English Gallery in Peterborough gave a family opening for the exhibition *The Williams Family, Yesterday and Today*. This brought together the sculptures of Sydney and Mary alongside Stuart's drawings. Sydney's work had not been shown in the twenty-two years since his death. Although Mary's horses and her riding lessons took up most of her day, she continued to sculpt table-size pieces but had not exhibited these in some years. A report in the *Jaffrey-Rindge Chronicle* described Stuart's work as "pen and ink sketches of flowers, animals and whatever he pulled from his active imagination." The flyer advertising the show was Stuart's drawing of three foxes in which a papa fox lectures two kits, "You two think you are so smart." The family gathered for the opening. All were in good spirits.

Two days later, on the night of December 2, Mary Williams died in her sleep. Stuart found his mother in the morning. He could not reach anyone in the family, so to calm himself he saw to his goats, then began another round of phone calls. This time he reached several of his brothers and sisters.

Before retiring the previous evening, Mary had begun a letter to George and his wife, who had been unable to come from Ohio for the opening. She recounted details of the event, the guests, the family who came and the family who couldn't make it, and described an early birthday party for Stuart. "Today is the day 22 years ago," Mary continued, "that papa died; the day when my world as I knew it came to an end & I had to begin to forge a new one centered around you children . . ." She expressed pride in all her

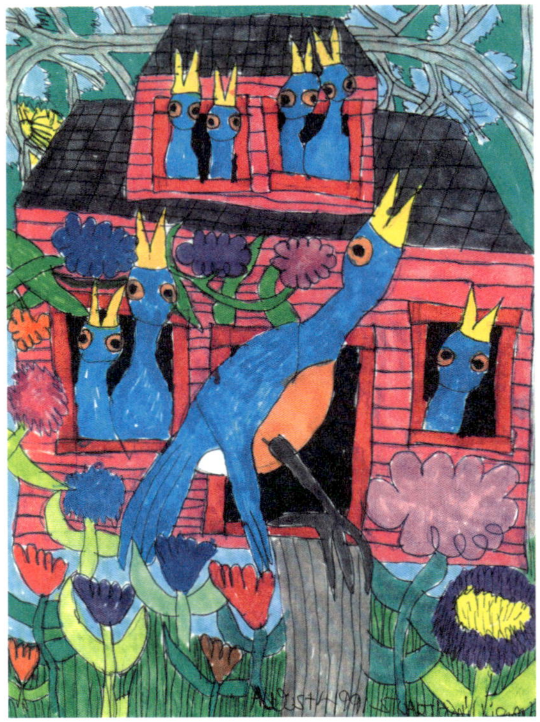

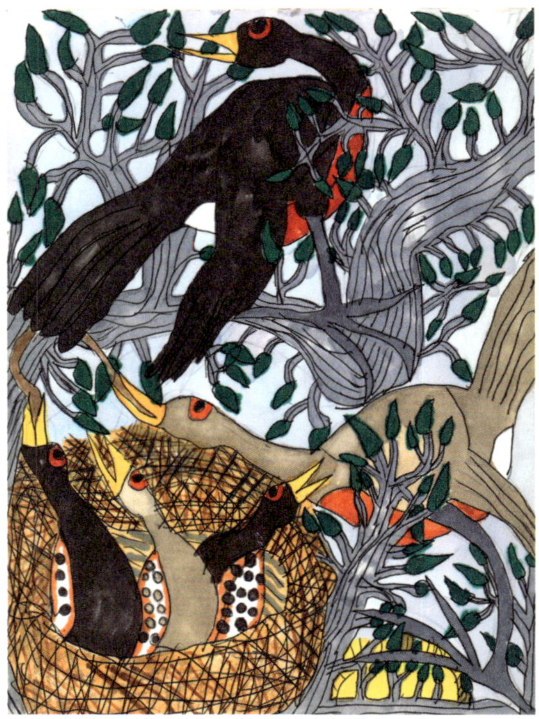

Bluebirds in a birdhouse, blackbirds in their nest and Stuart's portrait of a crow. Stuart painted birds found around his Peterborough home. They typically appear either grouped in nests or in portrait. He painted the crow on a scrap of slate (right).

children, then shared news about work on the Dodge Place before ending, "Tonight Stuart & I will celebrate his real birthday with a steak and some frozen dessert he bought plus broccoli & baked potato! He is cleaning his goat house in anticipation! I gave him a beautiful book of Audubon mammals! All the paintings & complete text unabridged! Also a copy of a photo of him with his [friend]..." The unfinished letter was found on her night table.

After the death of his mother, Stuart became, in his own words, "more and more depressed." Sue Martin, Frank's then-wife and a social worker, recognized this as a "critical time" for Stuart. Since no plan was in place for Stuart the family gathered to discuss how best to help him. His sister Betsy, a horsewoman like her mother who boarded horses and taught riding, and her husband Dick Moody volunteered to take Stuart into their New Boston, New Hampshire home. His stay lasted three months. Stuart later recalled that he "wasn't comfortable there. I was bored and they didn't trust me with food." Betsy found her brother totally unused to living with others. When he took a shower, it could last an hour, depriving everyone else of hot water.

Stuart returned to the Dodge Place and lived there with his dog Simon, but his depression deepened until a breakdown put him in McLean Hospital outside Boston—the fifth generation in the family, brother Sydney pointed out, to spend time there. Such was his condition that for the first time he was given antipsychotic drugs. There was a family meeting, leading to Stuart's admittance to a psychiatric hospital in White Plains, New York, near enough for Frank and Sue, who lived in Manhattan to visit. During that time Sue saw a lot of Stuart. To her he confided his suicidal thoughts and that he found it impossible to trust anyone. He had no interest in art.

The family is divided over how much the doctors who treated Stuart during these months knew about Prader–Willi. His siblings seem to have understood his disease each in their own way. All had observed firsthand his obsession with food and knew well his manipulative nature. But there was no family consensus on where Prader–Willi began and Stuart's responsibility for his behavior ended. Resentments were bound to surface, and they did. For his part, after his discharge from the hospital in White Plains, Stuart wanted to return to New Hampshire.

The family looked into family living situations in the Peterborough area. Frank remembers "driving him from White Plains to the first of these and meeting the family and looking around the place; it was the first and it seemed strange to leave him."

Soon after his mother's death, when Stuart was either at Betsy's or the Dodge Place, Kimberly Shaw, a framer and gallery owner in nearby Keene, unaware of his mother's death, offered him a one-man show. Stuart accepted, and his grief and the turmoil in his life spurred him to a period of intense work. "I used my art through hard times," he told the *Boston Globe*'s Gail Kelly. "It kept me from going insane." In a few weeks he finished more than seventy pictures, "frolicking," as he said, and unable to stop. Many pictures are dated 1991, but just which weeks he worked—between hospital stays or afterward—is difficult to determine.

The Shaw Gallery exhibition had such success, and

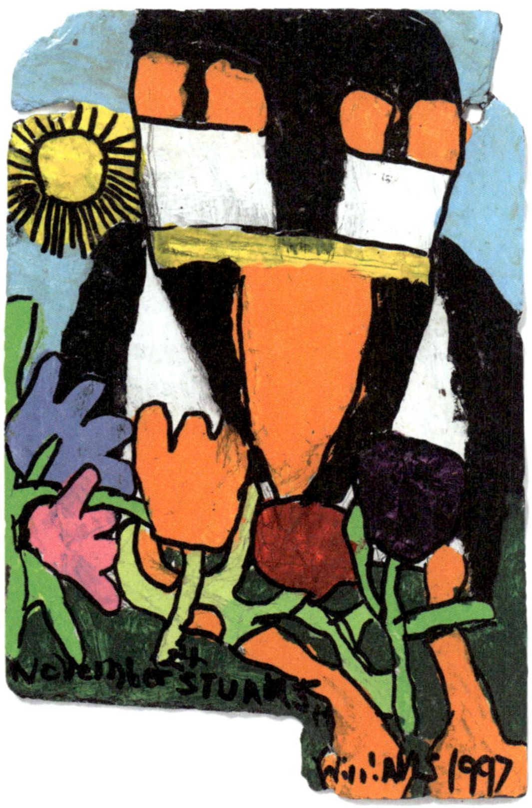

Stuart continued to produce so much art, that the gallery gave him a second show in 1992. He followed that with a show at the Cheshire County courthouse.

In March of that year, Stuart went to live in a group home run by Stuart and Julianne Weeks in Temple, New Hampshire. On February 4, 1993, with Stuart about to begin a second year in the home, Stuart Weeks sent the family a letter. His first purpose was to inform them of the "*astounding* struggle that flowed out of him [Stuart] yesterday" as he had written for ten straight hours. Before quoting from Stuart's pages, Weeks asked his siblings to keep foremost in their minds a question he had asked in other ways before: "What is at work in a *destiny*, can we say when the 3 most important people/creatures (ma, pa and dog) in a person's life *all* died on his birthday?"

Weeks wanted them to consider this fact as something more than coincidence. He asked that these deaths be understood as "integrally and intimately related to Stuart and to the real suffering and loneliness he has experienced..."

Stuart's writing began with the aftermath of his father's death and his feeling that "my weight problem became the focus for all the upsetness that lived in [my mother]." He described his reaction to Mary's death, his time with Betsy and the lack of trust he had felt in her house, his return to the Dodge Place and his life there with his dog, until Simon too died on his birthday. "I didn't know why," he writes, referring to the three fateful deaths. "I thought they were punishing me."

He ended by returning to food and trust: "But again they didn't trust me. A couple of times I ate more than I should have. I know it was wrong..." At some point or other, Stuart may have indicated as much to all of his siblings, but this is the only written record he left of his reaction to the deaths on his birthday. As a victim of Prader-Willi, his grief and complicated feelings of guilt are inextricably linked to his obsession with food.

Attached to Stuart's letter was a memo from Weeks dated July 3, 1992. Part I presented "comments" Stuart had made to Weeks over the preceding months. Stuart had revealed that as a boy he had been bullied and sexually abused by older schoolmates. He also said that for some time he had been hearing voices, including animal voices. "'I'm very angry with mother,'" Weeks quoted Stuart, "'in part because she wouldn't talk with me about things I really wanted to talk about, like how I am different from others and my constant battle with food.'" Stuart emphasized that he'd "rather die than be committed" to a mental hospital or facility for the care of those with Prader-Willi.

The Weeks letter ended with this exchange between Weeks and Stuart:

"Stuart, Dr. Wharton [an expert on Prader-Willi at Boston's Spaulding Rehabilitation Hospital] said that Prader-Willi people are always hungry. Are you always hungry?"

"No."

"When are you not hungry?"

"When I have eaten a good meal."

"Are there other times?

"When I am painting."

The following year, 1993, Stuart, still living at the Weekses', was the honored guest at the Prader-Willi Syndrome Association conference in Scottsdale,

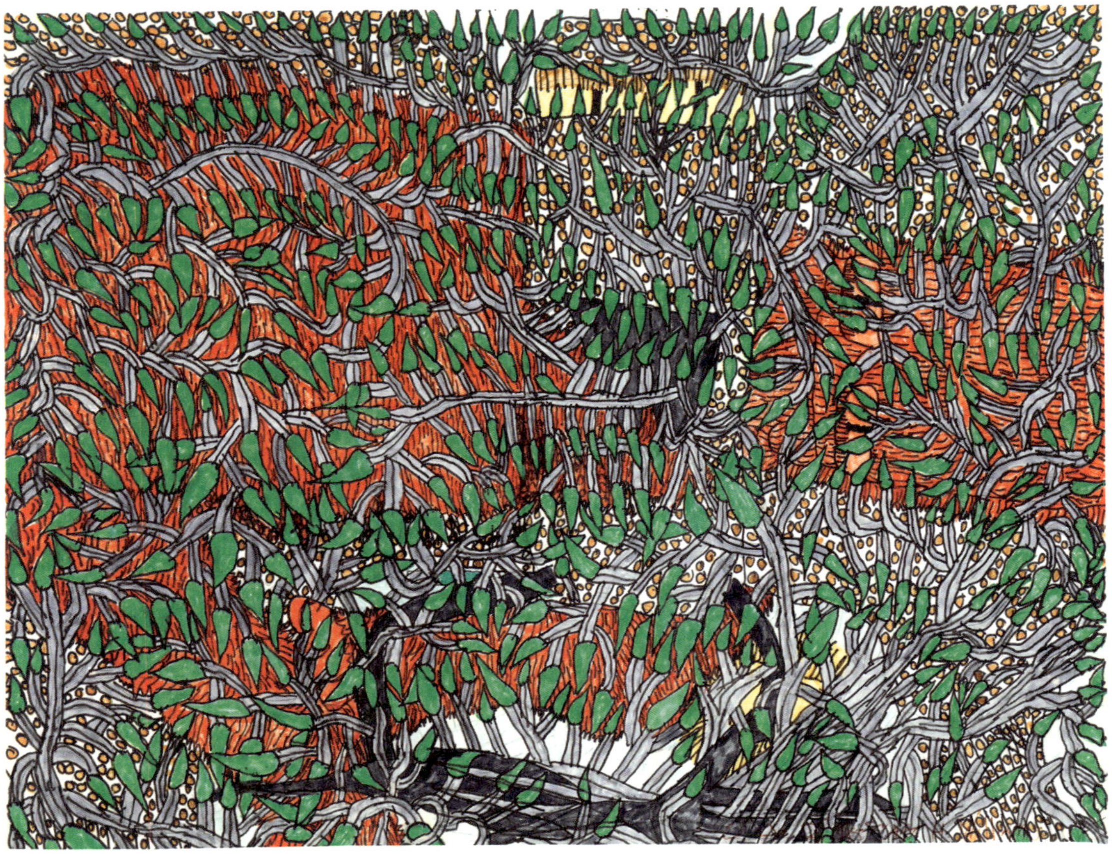

A dense late work in which Stuart protects the animals he loved behind impenetrable undergrowth.

Arizona. The Association billed Stuart as "a unique individual—animal lover, goat farmer, country music enthusiast, wildlife photographer, veteran of two African safaris—Oh, yes, a 42-year-old man with Prader-Willi syndrome." Stuart had become a poster boy, celebrated by an organization well aware of the odds he had overcome to live a life of accomplishment.

Sheldon Tarakan, publisher of *Prader-Willi Perspectives*, had prepared the way for Stuart with his "Portrait of an Artist," featured in the magazine. He interviewed Stuart in New Hampshire and photographed him feeding his goats, at work on a new painting, and displaying his art. Tarakan was struck, as so many were, by Stuart's rapport with his goats, his "non-verbal communication."

Stuart took care of his small herd of goats for a few more years. He kept them quartered at various farms not too distant from where he was living, but his herd came at a personal cost. Siblings and others remember that Stuart stunk of his goats, especially the rank and randy odor of the billies. The smell made it difficult to be around him. Since he depended on others for transportation, Stuart, who loved few things more than a road trip, got out less frequently.

In 1995 he had his last show of the decade, at the Connecticut Mental Health Center at Yale University. It was up during the summer to promote the Special Olympics. Family members recall the opening, but about the exhibition itself much is unknown. How many pictures were hung? Were they for sale? Was the show reviewed? Without Stuart to help fill in some of the blanks, we are left with just the unusual venue and an absence of information.

At the Weeks' home he had met and made friends with John Eisenman, a fellow boarder. This developed into the crucial relationship of Stuart's later life. Eisenman left New Hampshire in the mid-1990s but remained in close touch with Stuart by phone and was devoted to him. Over the next decade Stuart would move several times and live mostly in group homes or family situations. Toward the end of his time in New Hampshire, he resided for some months in a house Frank bought for him on Thorndike Pond in Jaffrey.

Stuart lived a semi-independent life, cared for and fed by various local agencies, including Perfect Peace and the Monadnock Redevelopment Services. Eisenman remembers him making art and being, most of the time, in fairly good physical and emotional

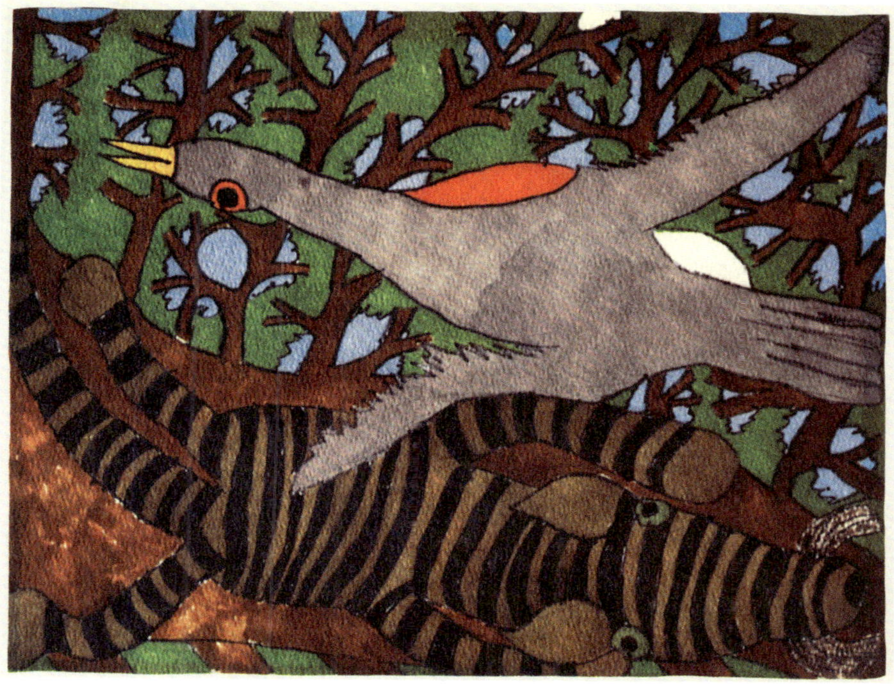

The Cat And The Robin, one of four postcards published under Stuart's Creature Prints imprint.

shape—sustained, Eisenman notes adamantly, by his strong religious faith. Stuart was not a churchgoer and had not been reared in a religious home. According to Eisenman, his relationship with God—intensely personal, and based on private conversations—had been arrived at on his own.

The strain of finding a barn for his goats, managing the commute to care for them, and his moving house himself several times caused Stuart to give up his herd in 1996. Goats would only rarely appear in his subsequent work.

Africa had taken him off the farm, opening up subject matter he now constantly returned to. Whales (he had been on several whale watches off the Massachusetts coast), dolphins, and various fish—certainly observed on nature DVDs—joined his cast of characters as well. He paid closer attention to flowers and leaves, often covering his pictures with dense foliage, and bees became prominent. He also became more concerned with environmental and habitat preservation issues. Over his last working decade (Stuart finished few pictures after 2007), in the story-like captions he wrote on the back of many pictures, the animals narrate their adventures in worlds that are growing complex and threatening.

After the Yale show Stuart's public art life pretty much took care of itself. His brother Frank had become an art collector, and dealers who came to see his collection naturally saw Stuart's art. In December 2003 his show at Boston's Nielsen Art Gallery opened during a blizzard, which did not dim Stuart's pleasure at his first one-man show in a commercial gallery. In 2006 he had a show at Manhattan's Davis & Langdale Company. Many of the pictures from those exhibitions are dated 1991, when he had been making work for the Shaw Gallery show, a year of furious activity for Stuart.

In the late 1990s, Stuart confided to Eisenman his desire to relocate to the Southwest or West, to escape New Hampshire's cold and icy winter dangers. He had no more specific idea where he wanted to go. Eisenman had moved to Tucson, and Stuart went for a visit, but Arizona didn't feel right to him. In 2000 or so, Stuart suggested Texas. Eisenman thinks this notion came to him, in part, from his deep love for country music. Researching Texas, Eisenman discovered Abilene. In the summer of 2007, Catherine Boyle, a friend and caregiver, drove Stuart west, the longest road trip of his life. She stayed in Abilene for several weeks helping Stuart to get settled.

Stuart's first Abilene home was a duplex where he was cared for by the staff of the Hill Resource Center. He got a dog a mutt, to keep him company, but when the dog barked loud and long, the neighbors called the police. Stuart had to give up the animal.

But bigger problems, depression and the insatiable desire for food, bore down upon him. During his last decade, Prader-Willi dominated Stuart's life. The medical records of these years are sad reading. Stuart was beset by suicidal thoughts. His refusal to take sleeping medication exacerbated these while arousing in him fears that his body was shutting down. He threw tantrums, refused to follow doctor's orders, fell and hurt himself, and began to order large amounts of food over the phone, including entire pizzas and gallons of sweet tea to be delivered to his home. What he didn't eat at once he stashed in a closet, probably fearing discovery and punishment.

Stuart fought his brother Frank, who had taken over responsibility for Stuart in the 1990s, over going into the Larry Hill group home, but in 2010 he finally assented, eventually moving into a commodious room with a very large, easily accessible bathroom in an alcove. John Eisenman contacted the Prader–Willi organization in search of information that might help his friend. "When I told whoever I talked to about Stuart," he wrote to Frank after Stuart's death, "they said that what he achieved was unusually amazing for someone with Prader–Willi." But this did not keep the end from being hard. Stuart now faced obstacles, physical and emotional, that he could not surmount.

It was in a Hill Resource Center home that I met and interviewed Stuart in March 2012, two months before his death. He was dressed in black and sat hunched over, with his chin on his chest. When he answered my questions, he lifted his head but did not look me in the eye. He spoke clearly and precisely in what I can only describe as a beautiful, melodious voice. He used a walker to get around, struggling to drag his heavy braces and boots.

Two days later I met him at "the Farm," a building on the outskirts of Abilene where Hill Center residents would spend time during good weather. We sat and talked, surrounded by other patients. He spoke enthusiastically of his love for country music and Johnny Cash, Charley Pride, and Tammy Wynette. He had just seen the Bellamy Brothers in concert. He told me he enjoyed nothing more than a car trip anywhere. (Others recall that he usually fell into a deep sleep immediately.) When I asked about his goats, he described them as "characters": "Each one different, can't remember how many." To his dislike of oil paint, he added that it was "harder to get what I want with it."

Through all his travails Stuart stayed alert to the natural world around him. An entry in his medical records observed him drawing longhorn cattle. Although I didn't see those pictures, in the field next to the Farm grazed horses belonging to Hardin-Simmons University, and Stuart told me he planned to draw these. I did see a few sketches of prickly pear plants, the ubiquitous local cactus similar to those that appear in Matisse's late collages.

The years in Abilene had wonderful moments, the most special of which was his attendance at a Willie Nelson concert. For the occasion, he had a country-style tuxedo tailored to fit and bought himself a broad-brimmed cowboy hat. He went with his sisters Charlotte, Betsy, and Jenny, sat in the front row, and applauded raucously, hooting and hollering so that Nelson dedicated a song to him. He had studio photographs taken (one of which is this essay's frontispiece). Stuart's smile is like a river.

On May 15, 2012, Stuart died suddenly in Abilene as a result of complications following hip surgery. He is buried in Peterborough's Pine Hill Cemetery near his Williams grandparents and his father and mother.

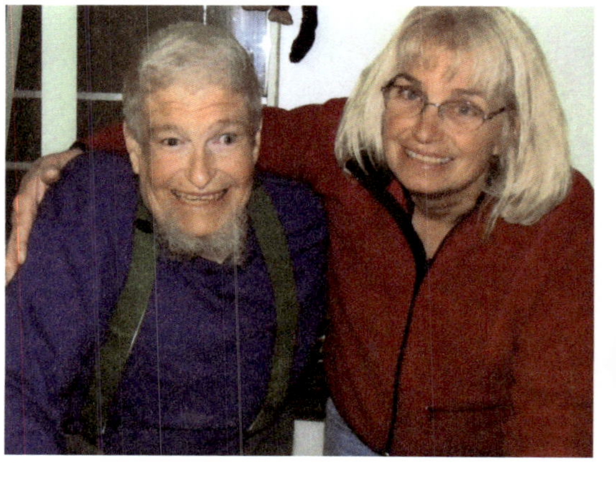

Stuart and his sister Jenny in Abilene, 2007.

Stuart completed two "Gisela" projects. In his late teens he wrote the fifty-four-page story "Gisela My Friend." The main character is the first registered Toggenburg doe kid that Stuart ever bought. He named her after his brother Frank's first wife, the German-born Gisela.

In 1967 or 1968, Stuart's first cousin Jody Hotchkiss visited the Dodge Place for a ski weekend. He was beginning his career as a literary agent, and Stuart's father gave him "Gisela My Friend" to read. Hotchkiss, who had observed Stuart with his goats and knew some of his goat drawings, responded very positively and asked to represent the story. Nothing came of his attempts to attract a publisher.

The second *Gisela* is a sequence of 273 drawings that tell Gisela's story. The images were unknown until discovered among Stuart's artworks after his death. Almost certainly made before 1981, these drawings are extraordinary for their high quality and a variety in composition sustained over what may have been only a matter of months.

"Gisela Eating My Sketchpad" recounts a foiled attempt to draw his goats from life, as Stuart is brought to tears by the naughty, rambunctious Gisela. "After Gisela had finished eating my picture," he wrote in "Gisela My Friend," "plus my pad, she saw me still sitting on the rock. She came to see what I was doing. But as she came to me, her head held high in the air, looking very happy, she reached up with her head and put it in my lap, resting it there, trying to make me feel better seeing tears in my eyes."

Although Hotchkiss's name and address are on one of the envelopes that held these drawings, they were never sent to him.

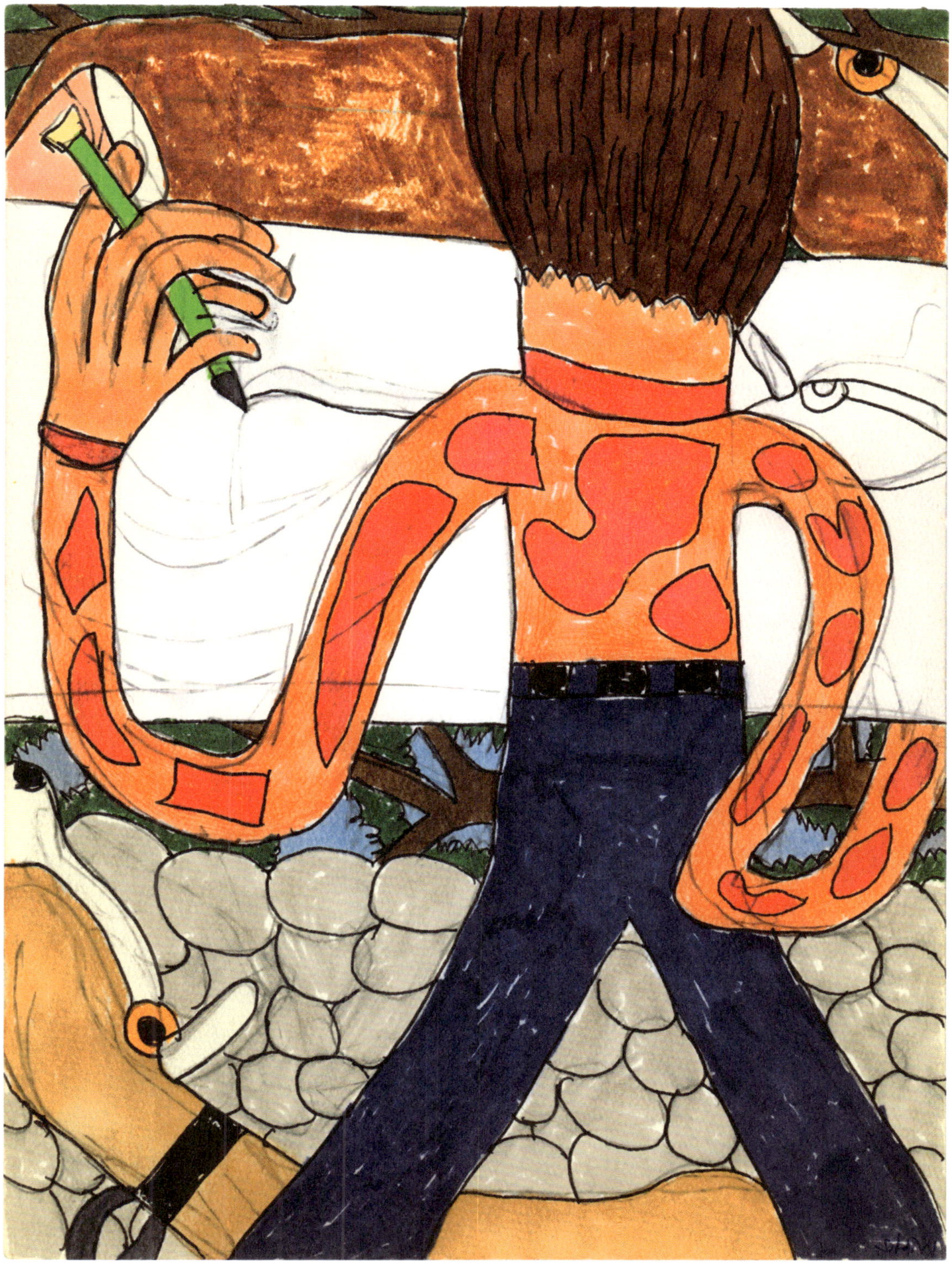

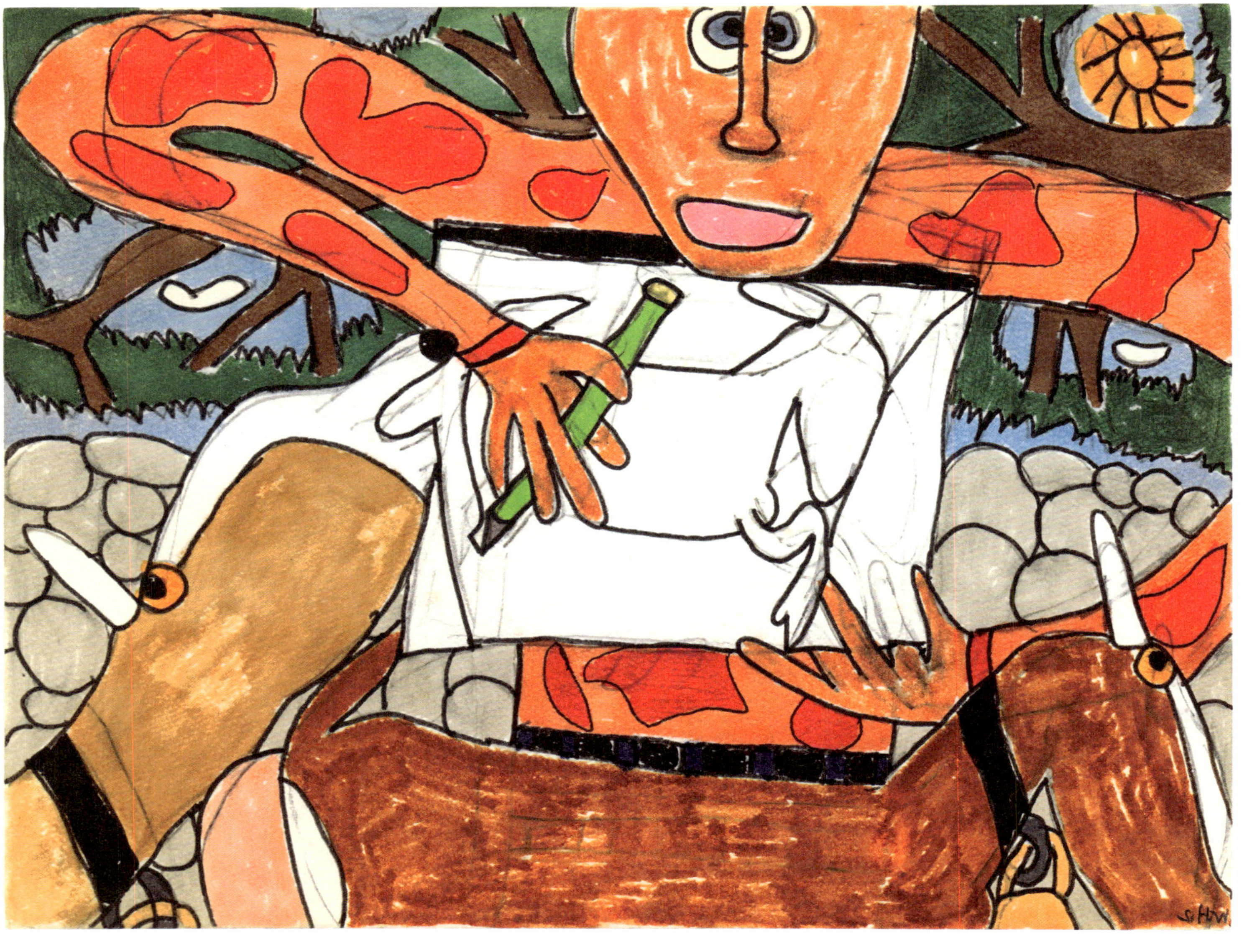

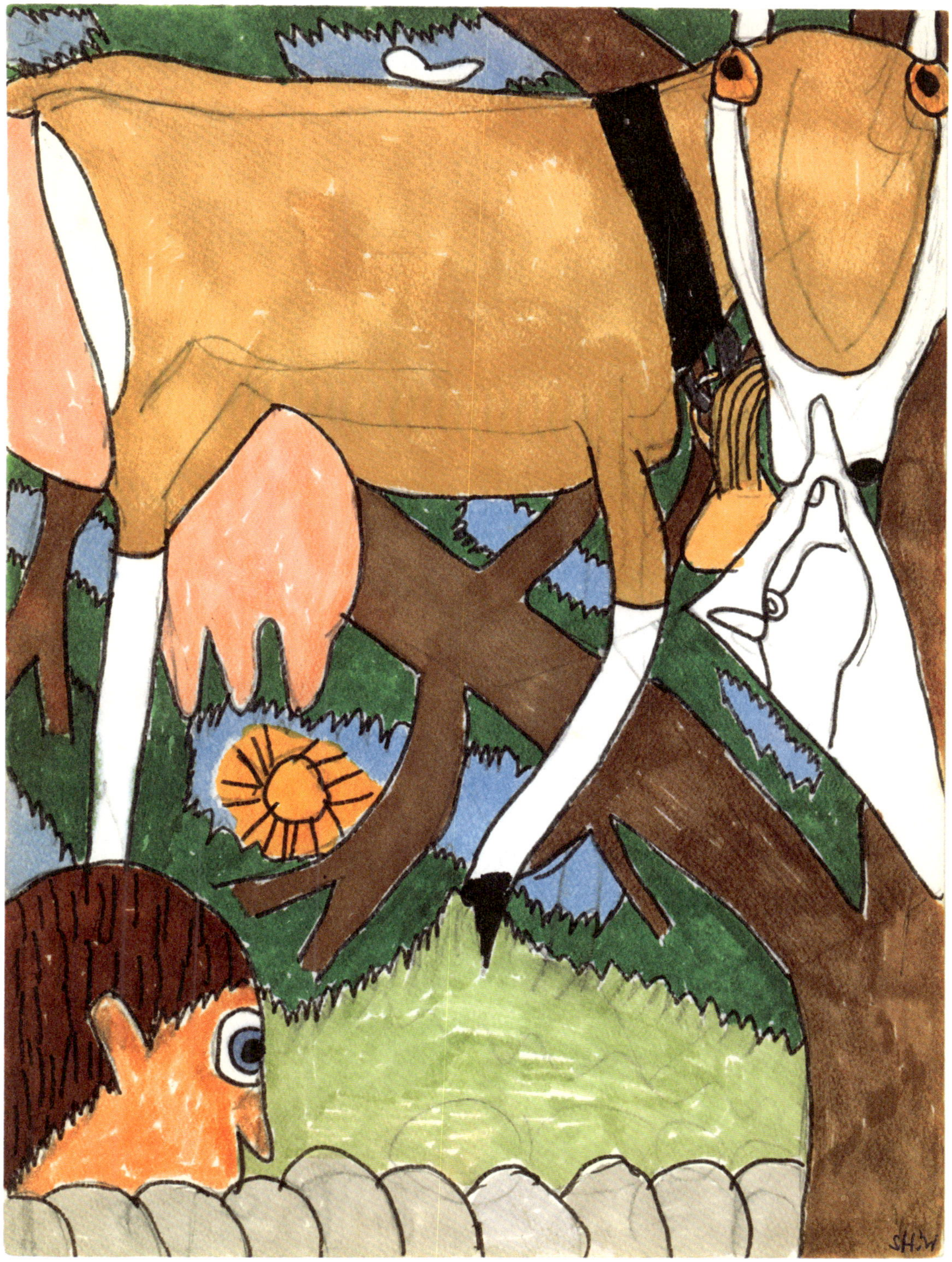

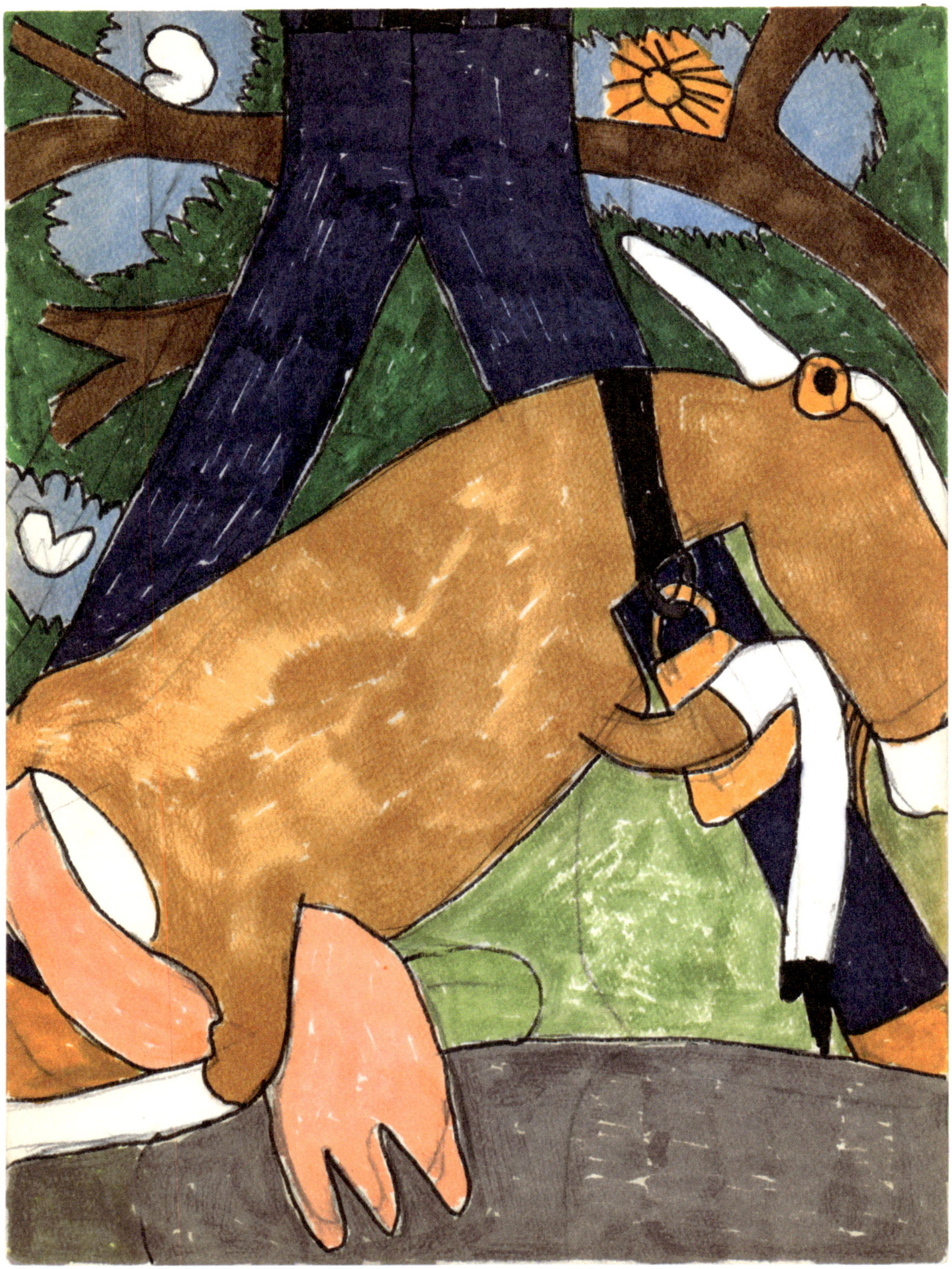

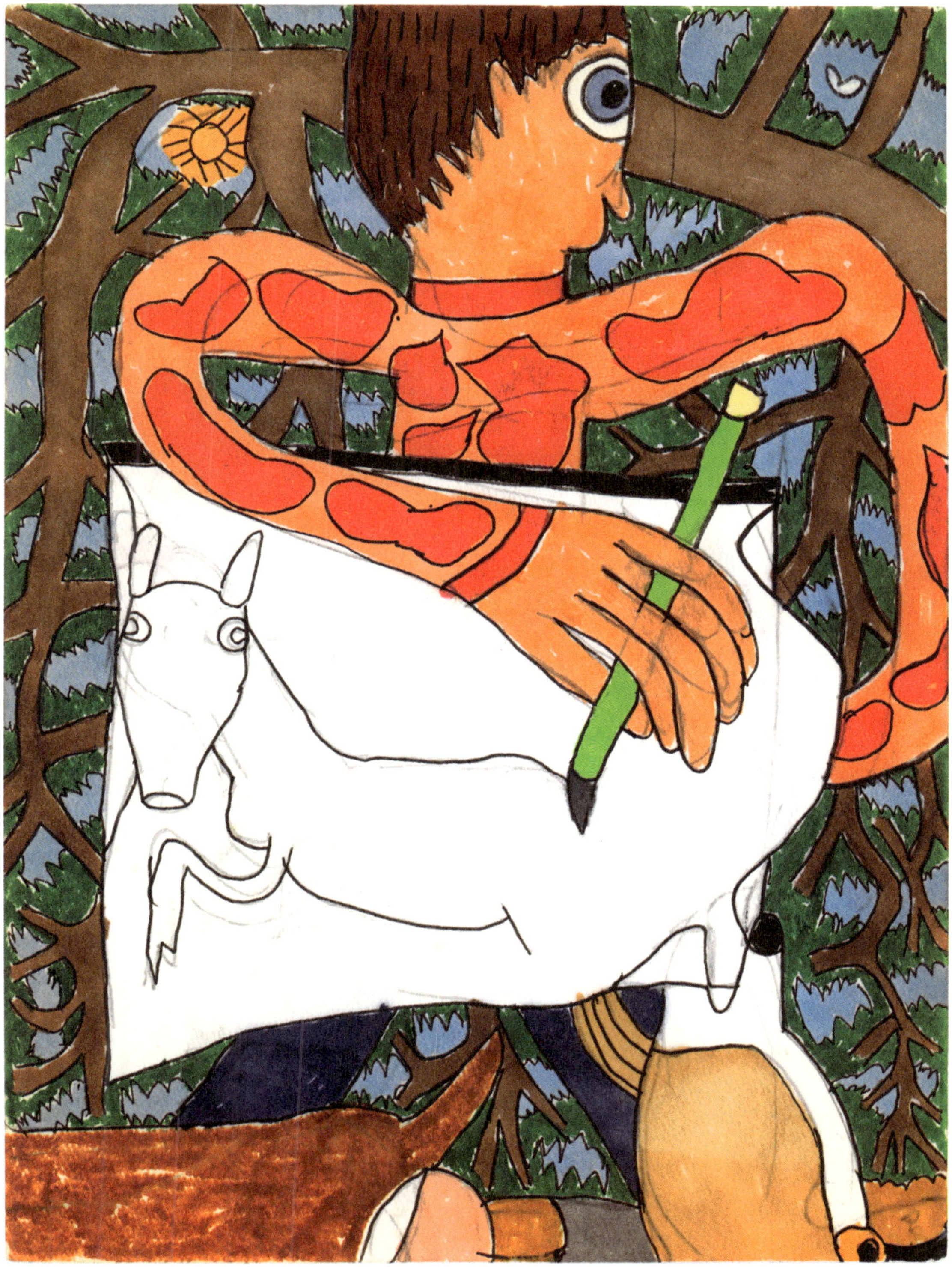

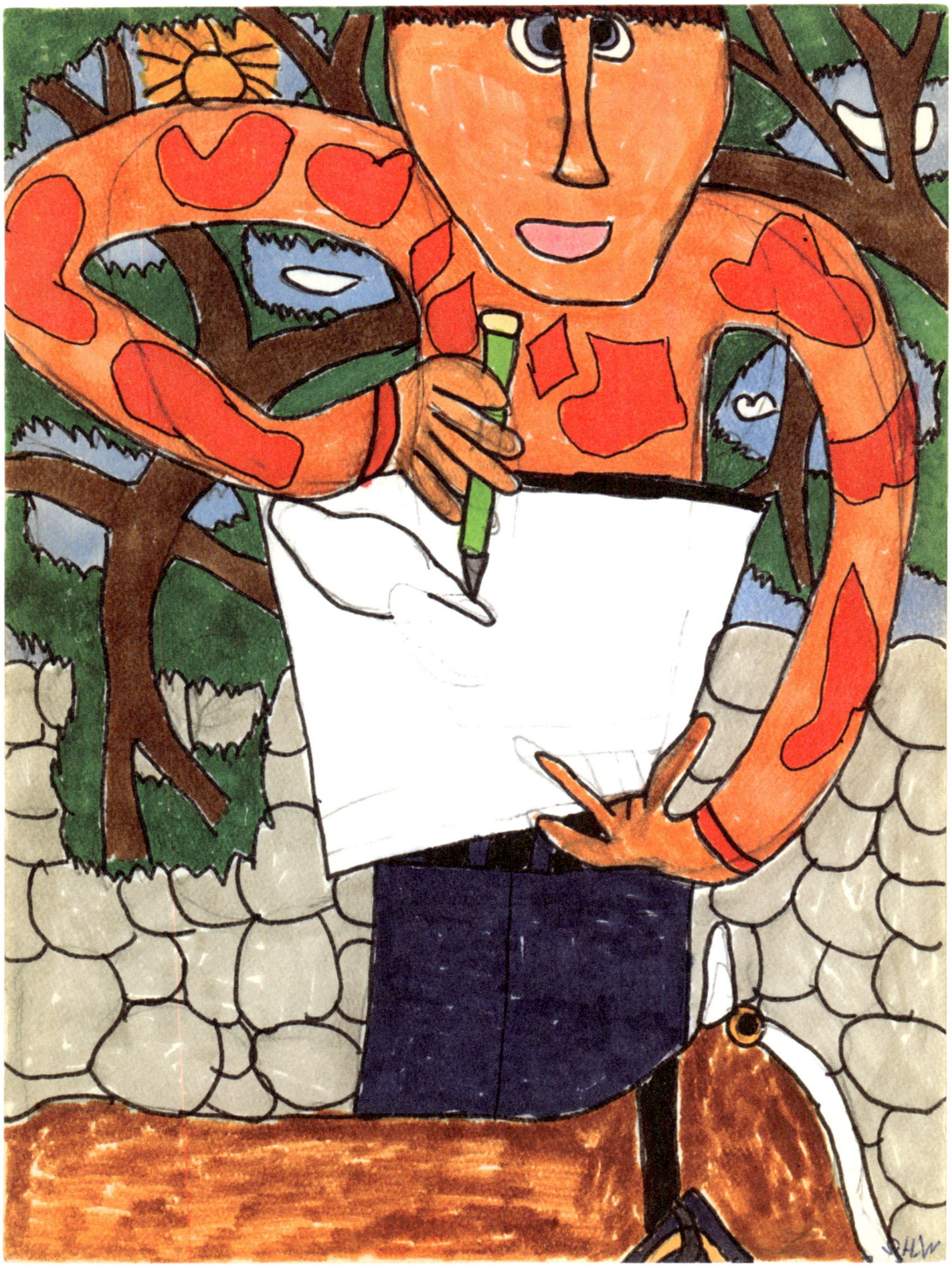

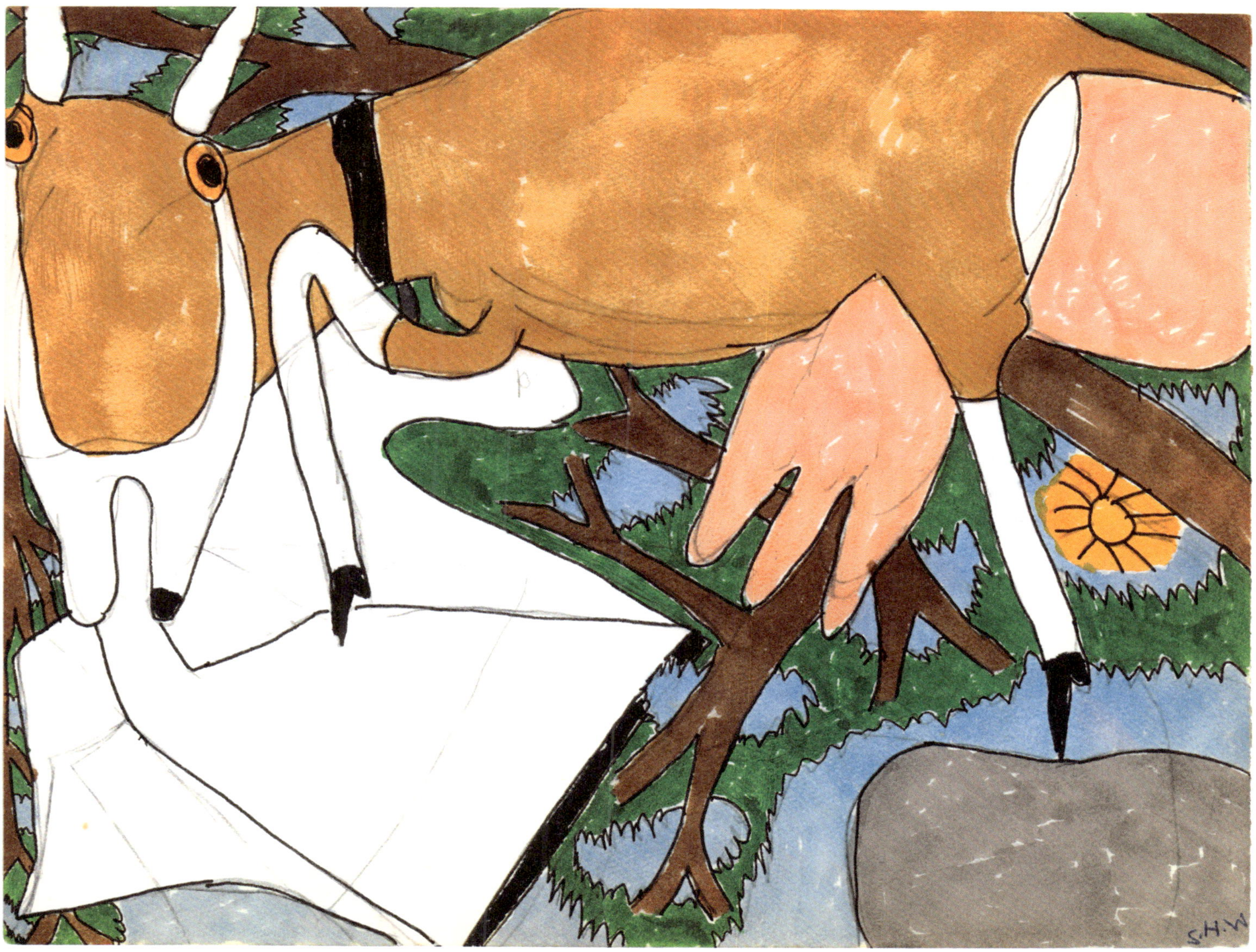
S.H.W

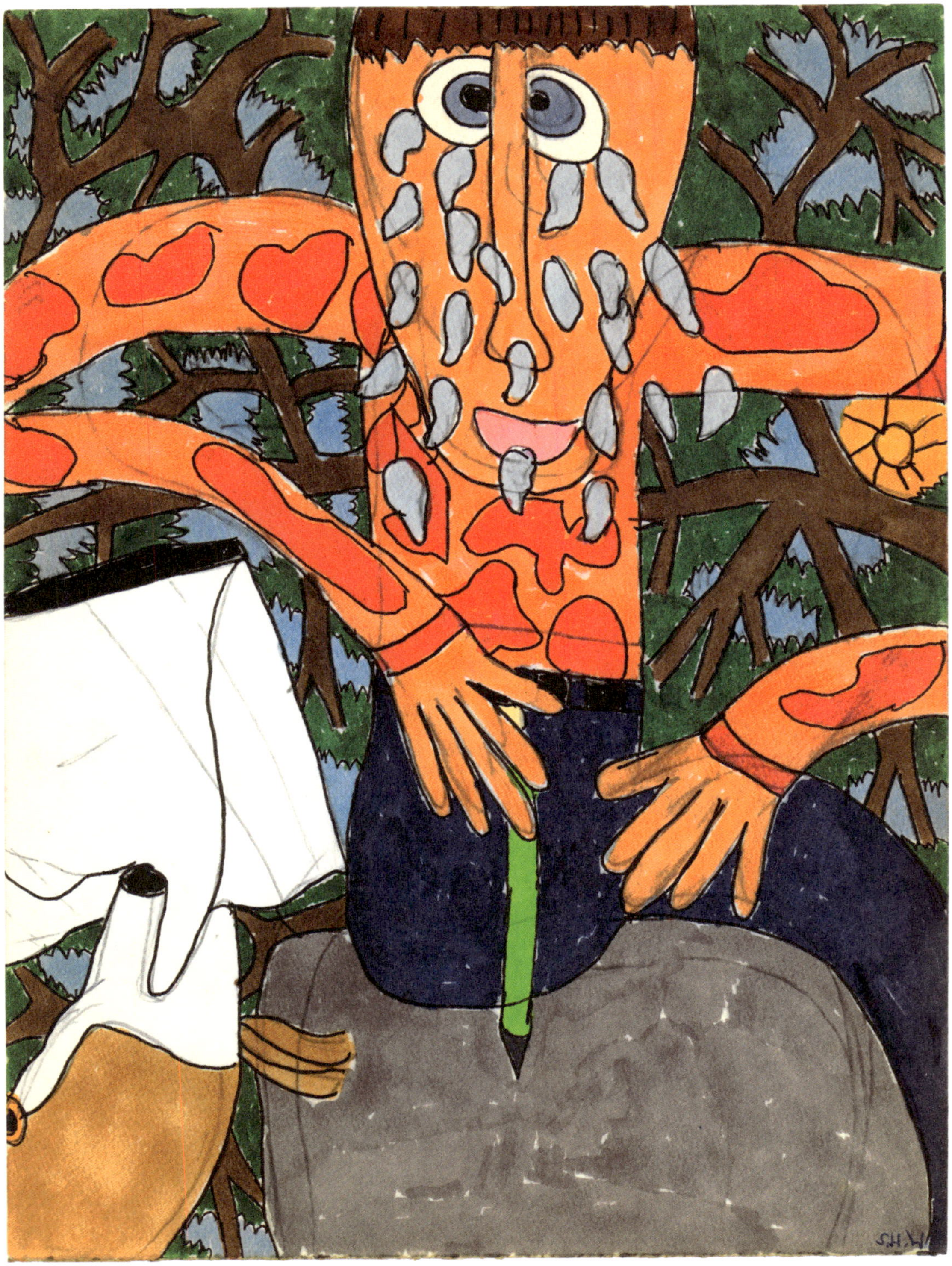

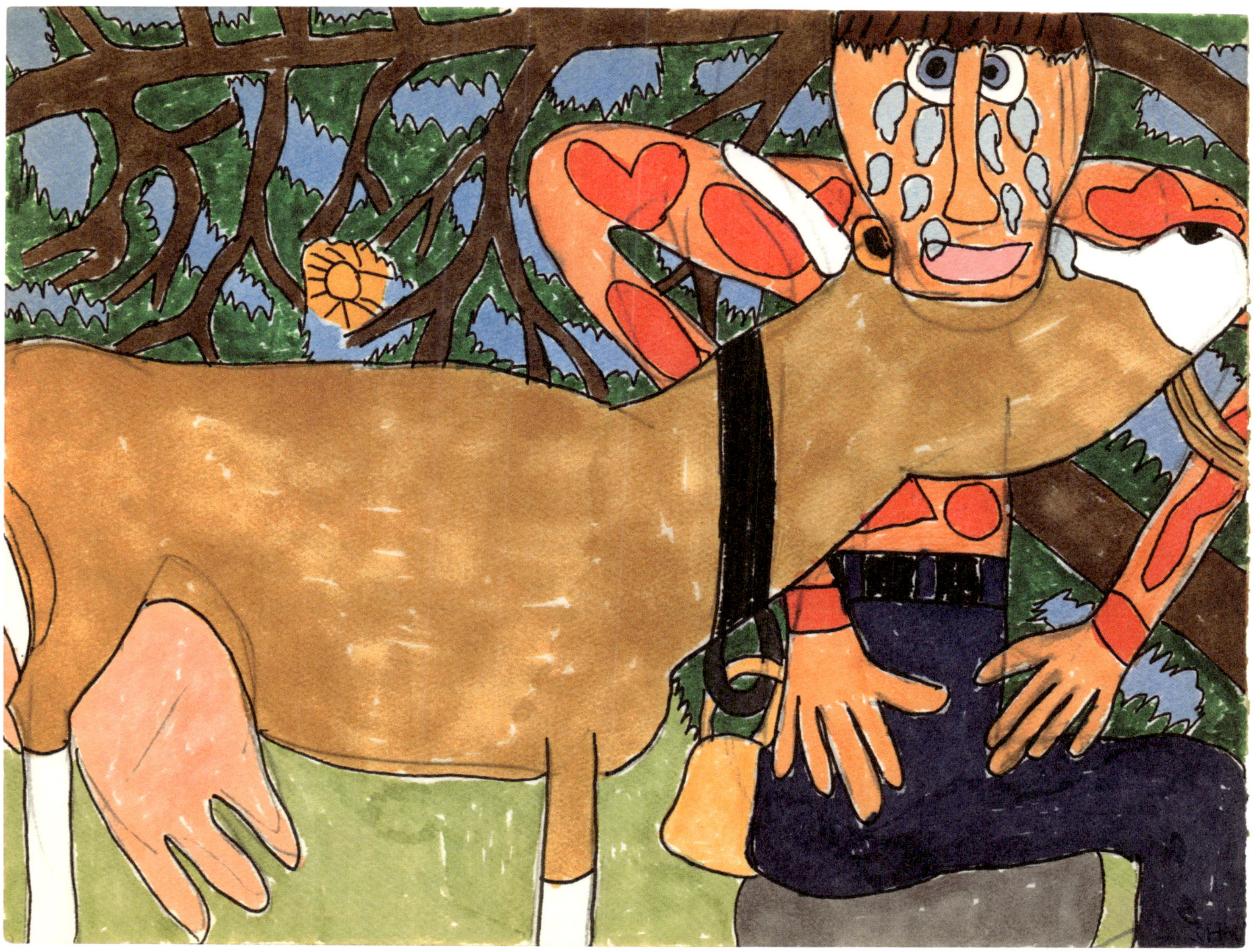

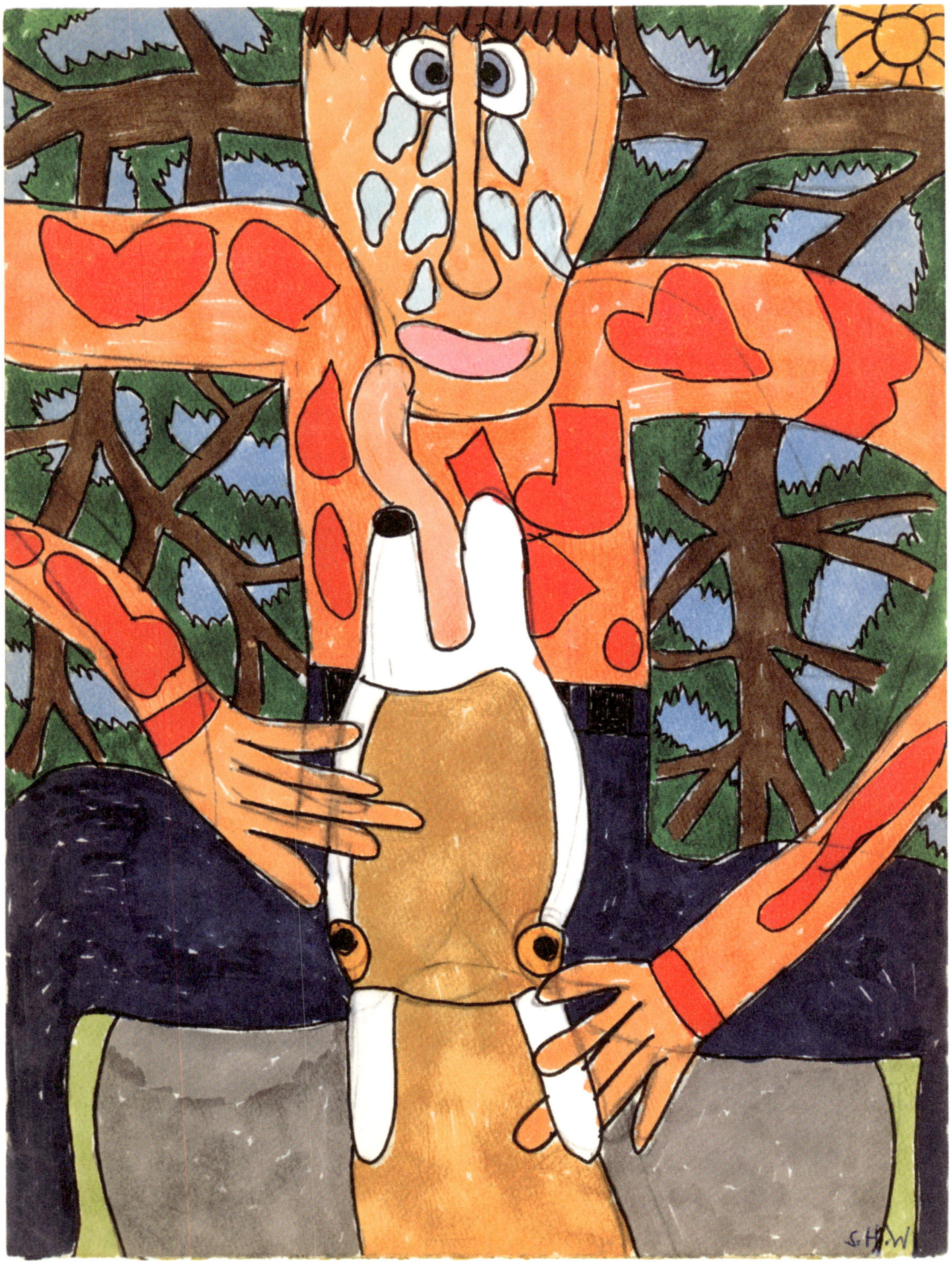
S.H.W

2 In her review of Stuart Williams's 2003–4 show at Boston's Nielsen Gallery, under the heading "Outsider Art," *Boston Globe* art critic Cate McQuaid wrote "Outsider art fails when its formal cleverness battles with its cloying naïveté, and that's the case here. Williams would be better served painting murals in youth centers or illustrating children's books."

McQuaid was too quick to identify Williams as an outsider artist. He was on record as pointing out that, growing up with artist parents in a home full of art materials, he had learned to draw by watching others. He had a practical school of instruction at hand and was hardly self-taught. At home and at the Gosling School, his talents were obvious and encouraged. During his early teens the artist and photographer Fleur Weymouth gave him two years of crucial lessons at the Sharon Art Center. In calling him an outsider artist in order to dismiss his work, McQuaid had Williams in the wrong ballpark.

By definition, outsider art comes out of nowhere. Williams participated in the art scene around him from his teenage years until his death. By his early twenties he had painted a mural and filled commissions for record covers and posters. His art had an enthusiastic local following and was collected.

Unlike so many outsider artists, Williams was not an ecstatic visionary inspired by religious feelings. Instead, he had, in his brother Frank's words, "a mystical connection with animals"; only later did he develop the intense relationship with God witnessed by his friend John Eisenman. Williams grew up on a farm, in a family devoted to horses. His parents, eager to add to their income, designed and manufactured a line of toy animals, Red Shed Rubber Animals, which they made into a successful, but very small, business. In modeling the more exotic animals, Sydney and Mary visited the famous Benson's Wild Animal Farm in Hudson, New Hampshire. All of the Williams children remember these trips and especially the antics of Benson's resident gorilla.

In the pasture behind the Dodge Place, Williams played for hours with these toys. His brother Willard remembers endless afternoons arranging and running farms with his brother. Stuart played with toy giraffes, gorillas, and camels long before he saw them in Africa. He gave each family member an animal identity:

Father Sydney: Big Chimp
Mother Mary: (unknown)
Mary: Big Elephant
Sydney Jr.: Bear
Frank: Lion
Betsy: Deer
Charlotte: Zebra
Jenny: Polar Bear
Stuart: Camel
Willard: Baby Elephant
George: Little Chimp

At around six years of age, Williams began to care for, grain, and milk a small herd of Toggenburg goats. He may not have known the anatomy of these animals as George Stubbs knew that of the horse, but Williams knew his goats intimately through his husbandry. His was not childlike devotion but serious adult work. In *The Dyer's Hand*, W. H. Auden invented an ideal curriculum for poets that includes keeping a garden and

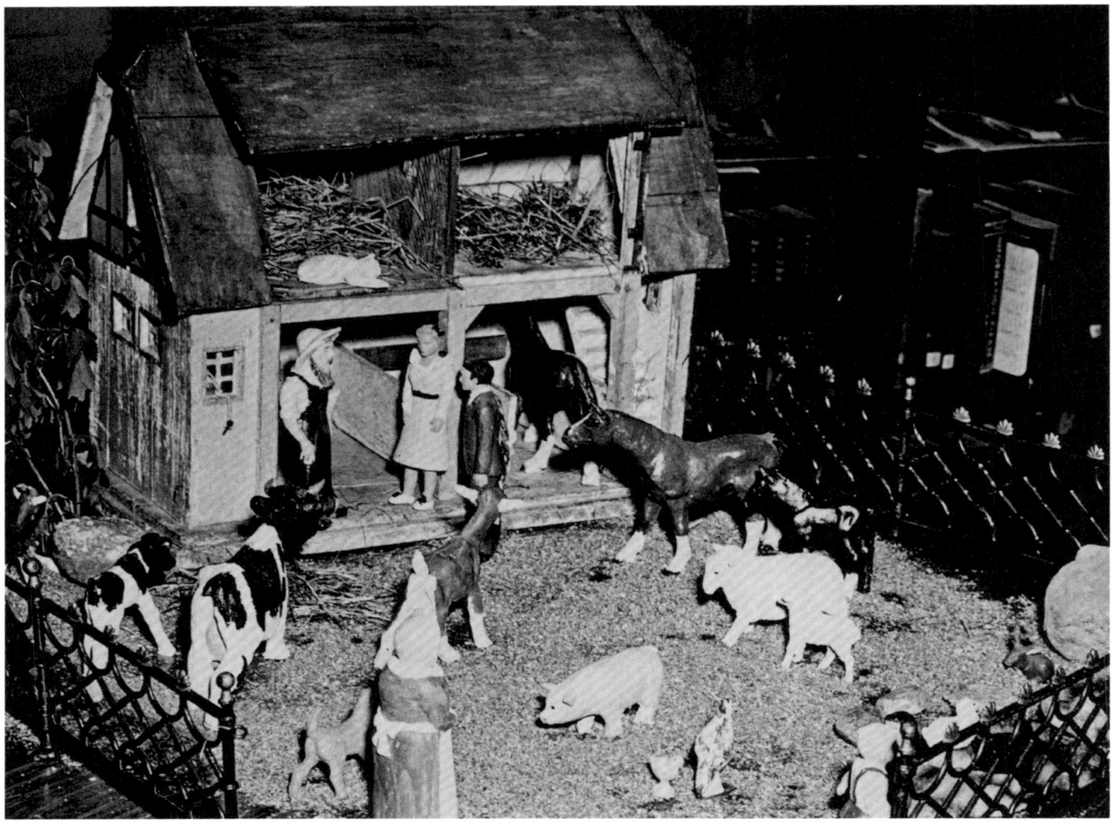

Red Shed Rubber Toys display. Photograph courtesy of the Monadnock Center for History & Culture.

raising an animal. Auden, who had no such training, argued that the discipline involved could not help but free an artist's sympathy and imagination from the limits of self. He could have used Williams as proof of his notion.

If Williams had a cause in his art, it was animal rights and, increasingly over the years, the health of our environment. This can be read in the story-like captions on the back of many of his pictures and is especially emphasized in those he made following his two African safaris. In Tanzania and Kenya, Williams traveled through game preserves in vans, looking out at the animals they passed. The pictures recalling those trips wittily depict humans looking out the van's windows as if from behind the bars of a cage. These works both ask who is being observed and suggest the strangeness of a self-appointed "higher species" gawking at creatures superior in grace and beauty. In numerous early farm pictures, animals look out at the viewer as if in wonderment at those who would look at them.

The *Globe*'s McQuaid also fell into a common trap: since Williams's art didn't look like high art to her but like folk art—homemade, unrefined, and absent of pedigree—the label *outsider* must apply.

Williams's champion Mac Doty saw the pictures differently. "[Williams's] color," wrote the curator, "and use of line define his forms and shapes which are arranged within the frame and plane of the image in a most extraordinary manner, not unlike cubism." Doty had his schooled yet unconventional eye peeled for what may not have looked like art. In the case of the first poster by Williams that he saw, the figures may, compared with his other work of the same time, have had a bumptious, funky appeal that he connected with folk art. By including Williams in the Currier show *By Good Hands: New Hampshire Folk Art*, he supplied a context for his art. Folk art—whether paintings, weathervanes, or billboards—is public art and has a purpose beyond self-expression. In the end this category is too narrow for the art of Stuart Williams, but the connection to it is evident.

In Williams's early work, animals he would have seen near his home in New Hampshire disport themselves, scattered across more or less realistic landscapes, as in the early painting he gave Bea Orchard, one of his teachers at the Sharon Arts Center. On the cover of Dudley Laufman's 1981 record album, cows dressed as Morris dancers gambol on a country church lawn. Stuart's sense of play was evident early on, and it

Album cover by Stuart, based on his concert poster for folk musician–poet Dudley Laufman.

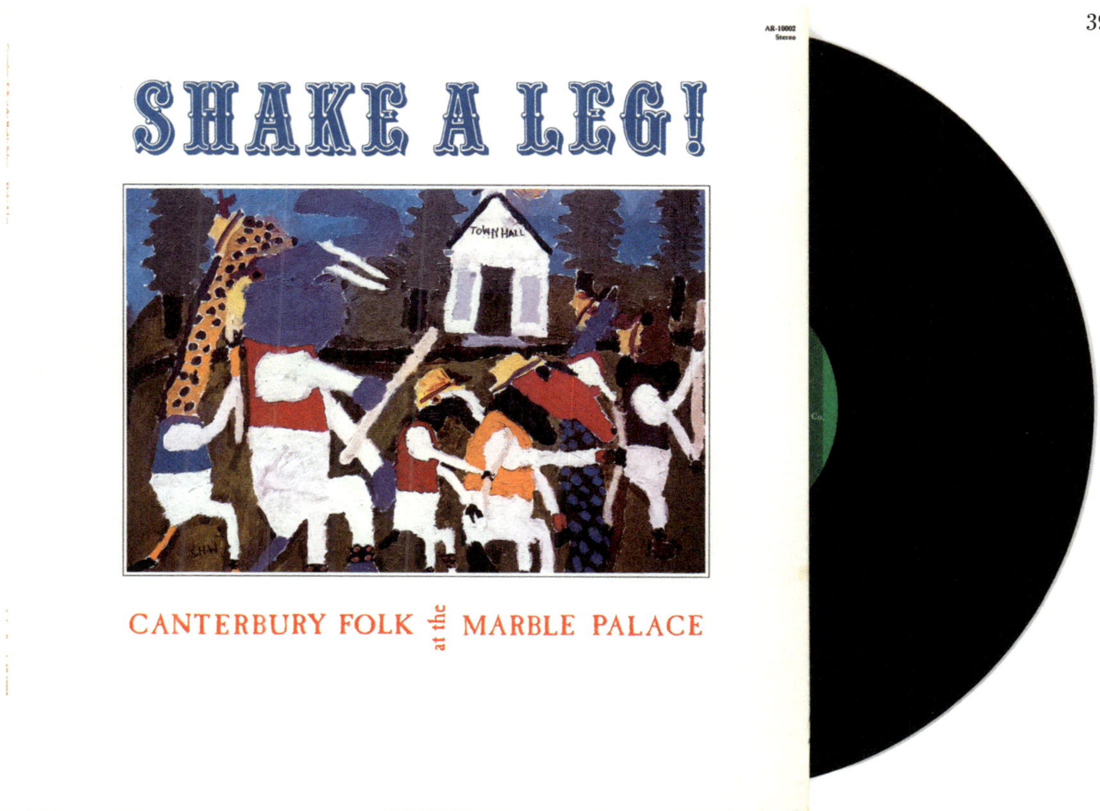

stayed with him even in pictures where a mock stern, bearded farmer, the artist himself, keeps his goats in line. His pictures, regardless of his psychological state, are rarely dark.

Flowers appear in early works until the 1980s, and later they dominate pictures. Williams liked them in the foreground with animals behind them peering out at the viewer. (Animals looking out warily at the viewer as if from hiding are a theme of Williams's art.) He loved a four-petal tulip shape—like an upright hand—but assured me that his flowers were made up and that he liked them all. He liked a sunny day too, a child's sun, bold and yellow, shooting out rays. There are a handful of night and winter pictures, but the typical Williams weather is summery and bright, the sky untroubled, as bees, big and slow, graze in the gardens and the animals are free in their play.

When Williams found a subject he liked, he returned to it through numerous variations, executing all his pictures in the same paint-by-numbers way. He began with the grid format that Fleur Weymouth had taught him. At his death he had a stack of poster board with the more elaborate grid that characterized his later work completed or in progress. Using this grid to orient himself, he drew in animals, foliage, and humans. His composition and outline complete, Williams used Berol markers to color in the figures. He liked to have an array of markers to choose from and often spent up to a thousand dollars to replenish his supply. Sometimes his brother Frank sent him a box of assorted colors from Pearl Paint in Manhattan.

Because Williams was unselfconscious when at work, several people have spoken of watching him make pictures. He could work on any flat surface, and although he had several studios over the years, he could, and did, work while in bed. Later he came to prefer a drawing table he could tilt toward himself. Sharon King, his primary caregiver through his last years, remembers Williams having to be in the mood to work, and that when he was drawing a grid or coloring one in, he became so absorbed in the detail of his pictures that a relaxed, peaceful look transformed his features.

Even in his youth, other artists did not inspire Williams. He had no interest in visiting galleries or museums, and he did not have art books in his library. In Abilene, I asked if he had a favorite artist. He took his time before answering, "Grandma Moses." It is likely that he saw her work only in reproduction in *Life* magazine. Two days later Williams told me he had thought of another artist then forgotten his name.

Creature Art price list hand-annotated by Stuart, who kept a sharp eye on his prices.

If he had no background in art history, Williams could rely on actual animals and the lives he imagined for them. He also had movies, which he loved, all kinds; although he did hate *Bambi* and movies in which animals were cruelly treated. He hated anyone who harmed animals.

From an early age, he loved books. His favorite road trips took him to used bookstores. He didn't buy one or two volumes but stacks of them, a dozen or more at a time, remembers his then-sister-in-law Sue Martin. As a boy he loved the Dr. Doolittle stories, as did his siblings, and the works of Thornton Burgess and Albert Payson Terhune, whose anthropomorphized animals had great appeal for Williams. His room in Abilene held a six-foot-wide floor-to-ceiling bookshelf filled with books, most on natural history or about specific animals, which remained passionate interests. Another, smaller shelf held DVDs and his country music favorites. Williams may never have watched a nature film while browsing through a nature book inviting his imagination to wander, but his Abilene room, with a comfortable chair in front of his television and books nearby, makes it easy to imagine this multitasking.

When I met him, he had, in a shoulder bag he carried, his current reading, a large picture book on gorillas. Since his African trips, they had appeared in his work, often looking cautiously through jungle foliage. His reading introduced him to Jane Goodall, and in Abilene he attended one of her lectures and had his photograph taken with her.

His family, animal lovers themselves, gave him every opportunity to see animals in their natural habitats. Sister Jenny took him to Switzerland and Africa as well as whale watching off the Massachusetts coast. He loved the water, loved to swim in rivers and streams. Water soothed his sensitive skin, and swimming may have given him his only experience of gracefulness. For a time he drew dolphins at play. Often droll about business matters, Williams told his brother Frank that since his dolphin pictures sold like hotcakes he planned to paint a few more.

Williams loved the money he earned from his work but, early on, seemed to have no business sense. He kept his prices under a hundred dollars, only raising them slowly at his mother's urging. When he opened his "Creature Art" gallery, he published a price list, later revised upward in his own hand. Having no favorites among his works, he was open, his family remembers, to selling any of them. On my visit to Texas, I looked through the few finished pictures Williams had in his room.

"Would you sell me this one?"

"Yes."

"How much are you asking?"

He gave me a shrewd look as if measuring my bank balance. "Three hundred dollars," he said in a crisp, no-bargaining tone.

Nina Nielsen proved to be as good a piece of luck for Williams as Mac Doty had been. She knew Frank Williams as a collector, had sold him a few pictures, and was visiting his Wellesley home to see his collection when she spied her first work by Stuart. Her interest was immediate. "Your brother? How many pictures has he done? Is he still working? Would he want a show?"

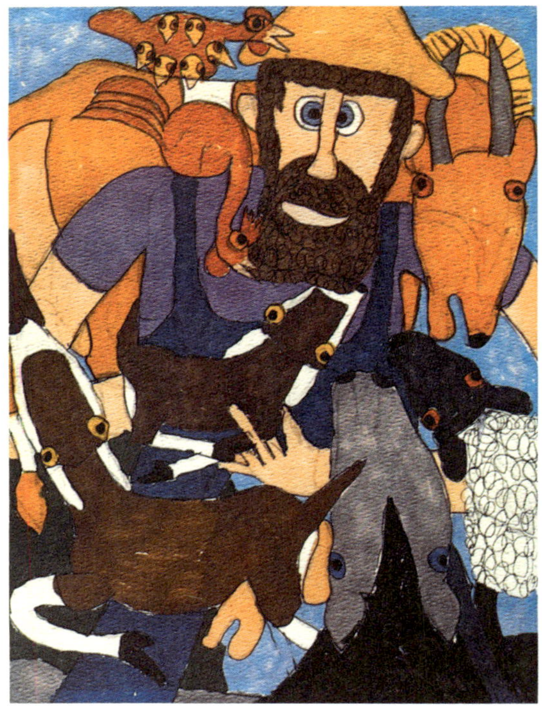

I'll Catch You Later, one of four postcards published under Stuart's Creature Prints imprint.

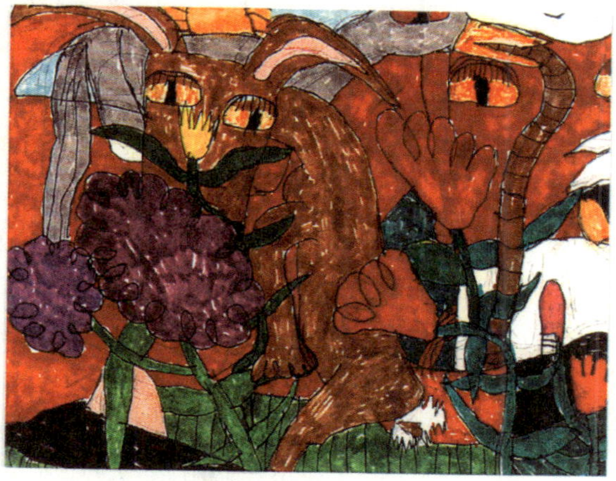

Creature Art

By Stuart H. Williams

POST CARDS EACH 50¢

CARDS $2.25 EACH

Framed and matted originals done with Berol Prismacolor markers

Originals	1 – 7	$680
	~~8 - 11~~ 9 - 12	$480
	12 – 17	$340
	18 - 52	$240

Acrylic Paint on Canvas

53 - $275
54 - $500
55 - $275
56 - $275
57 - $150

MINITURE
$100.00
~~$25.00~~
$125.00

Matted & unframed Originals

Mixed Media $100

Unmatted originals

Berol Prismacolor markers & color pencil	9x12	~~$100~~ $200
	11x14	~~$150~~ $250
	14x17	~~$175~~ $275
Mixed Media	14x17	~~$140~~ $210

Signed by the Artist Laser Prints

Small Prints	$10
Large Prints	$15

All other pieces are marked individually

As soon as Williams agreed, Nielsen arranged a show in December 2003 of eighteen pictures, dated from 1991 through 1999 and all but one titled "Gorilla eating a banana," with Williams's signature hand-printed back-of-picture captions. I happened to attend the exhibition opening; despite the blizzard sweeping Boston, it was a full house. Stuart's family recalls his delight at seeing his work on the gallery walls, and his even greater delight when sales were brisk.

Roy Davis and Cecily Langdale also discovered Williams's work through Frank, who handled his affairs after 1996 and championed his work. In working with him on his show at their Davis & Langdale Company in 2006, Davis found Williams to have "strong feelings about things" and be "much more aware of the art world than you might think, *not* naive at all." Langdale felt he had an "edge to him, gregarious, a little crafty."

Having bought a picture from the Nielsen exhibition, the collector Joanne Soja now bought another work by Williams from Davis and Langdale. Smitten by his feeling for animals, she thought him the right artist to paint a portrait of her beloved dachshund, Lucy, and engaged him in a commission. When the picture arrived, she searched for her dog in the thick grass and flowers. She summoned Davis and Langdale to look too. They could detect no dachshund. Well, perhaps a tail, but they were not certain. Queried, Williams responded that the dog's tail, pronounced as is common with the breed, was visible to him, but he coyly did not say where to look.

After his mother's death, Williams, beset by physical and emotional difficulties and having entered the world of professional caregivers, was often urged to forgo his art and apply his talents to more practical ends. Reluctantly, out of politeness or for other reasons, he went along and decorated trivets, serving trays, lazy Susans, wooden boxes, and plastic and wooden garbage cans. He deployed his signature four-petaled tulips, his goats, and other animals. Diana Shonk, who discovered his work at a local crafts fair, stores her winter gloves in what could be a breadbox resplendent in giraffes. Brother Willard, a bookseller, keeps inventory cards for his Toadstool Bookshop in a small wooden box decorated with flowers and foliage, and several other relatives have gaily painted plastic wastebaskets.

When the art Williams had in storage in Texas arrived at his brother Frank's Wellesley, Massachusetts, home after his death, one box revealed three T-shirts. These are stiff with paint, wearable but uncomfortable and of dubious commercial value. Williams also painted at least one clock face, and other examples of such "practical" art will doubtless come to light. Williams didn't work with the shapes of these household items but merely applied his images to them. Although the results are amusing, the objects are of interest only because he did them—you don't feel his heart was in it. They never displaced his art.

His postcards, Christmas cards, note cards, and especially his 1976 calendar are much more representative of his talent and imagination. The calendar is a major work, strong in composition and, because it was printed with the offset lithography process, bold and drenched in color. His animal and human figures have a supple, cartoonlike quality. July—"As you see here the horse is driving the man"—is special for its humor

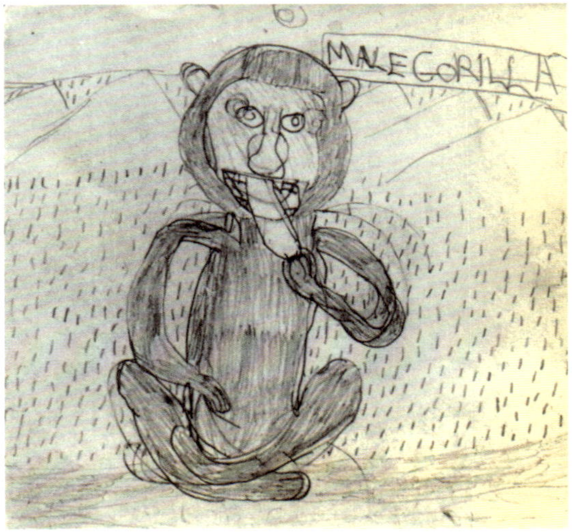

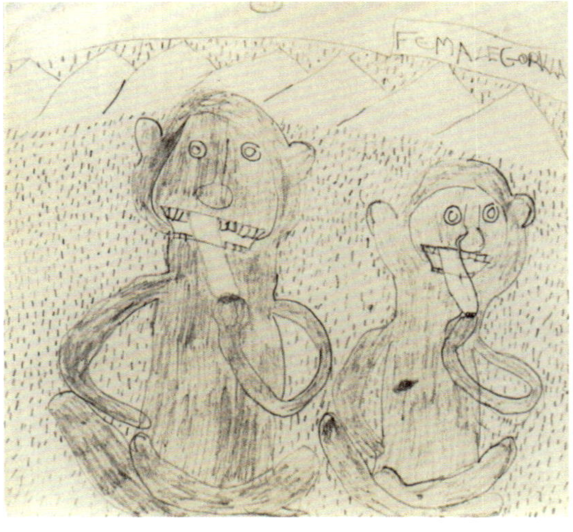

Two pencil drawings of gorillas found in a portfolio of late and unfinished Stuart drawings. At the time of his death Stuart was reading a book about gorillas.

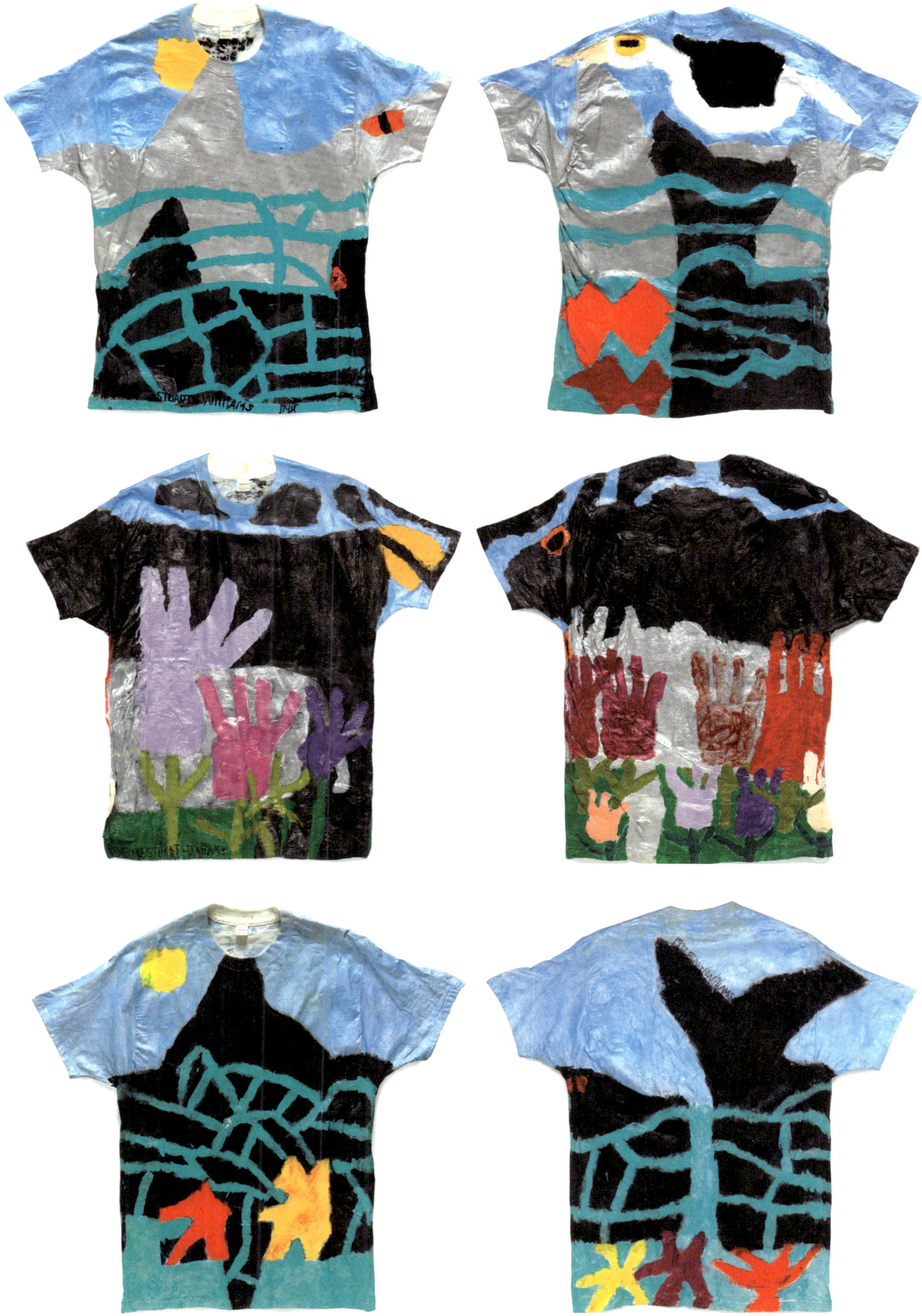

Stuart painted these T-shirts in Abilene. Like his painted trays, lazy Susans, wastebaskets, and note card boxes, they are one of his periodic attempts to produce items that could be sold in gift shops.

The months of Stuart's 1976 calendar, *Noah's Ark*, his last. In his note he explains that he skipped 1975 because a friend could not help him with the calendar.

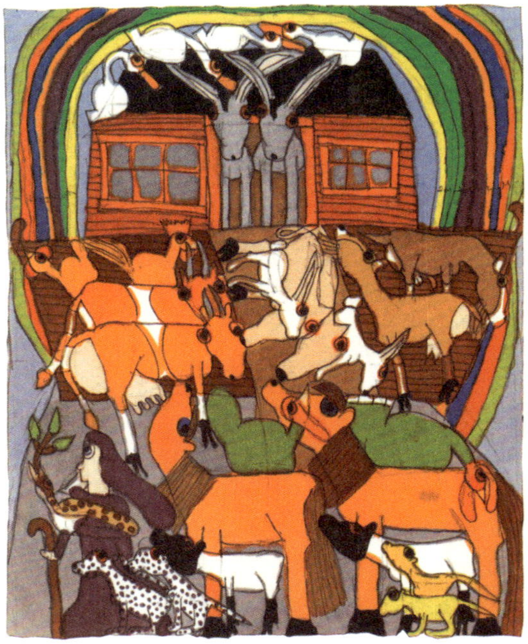

A postcard of the *Noah's Ark* painting used for the cover of his 1976 calendar.

and for what it suggests about Stuart's relationship to animals. After all, he had to get up every morning to serve his goatherd. This is a first-rate stand-alone work, but because Williams had no method of distribution beyond Peterborough's Toadstool Bookshop, only a few examples reached the public.

Among the other oddments that surfaced after his death are two rough, painted clay sculptures, a turtle and a panda. For a time, Williams's pictures of pandas excited buyers as his dolphins had. The sculptures may have been an attempt to come at his audience from a different angle or done at the urging of one of his caretakers.

There are several paintings on irregular-shaped pieces of slate that may have been roof tiles, fallen from a school near the Dodge Place. These are thickly painted, usually single images. They have a signlike quality and appear more closely related to folk art than anything else in Williams's body of work; while not a main attraction, they are arresting. At his funeral and the reception afterward, a number of these slates were displayed, and they stood out.

As a record of the work of Stuart Williams, this book is incomplete in one regard. Stuart dated and signed his work beginning in 1986 for the Currier show. Before then, his pictures are undated and unsigned. He attended to these professional facts of life when the larger art world required them, but prior to that they had no importance for him. It would be interesting, for example, to know when the bearded farmer began to appear in his pictures. The goatherds in the 1976 calendar are boys. By 1991 the farmer, a self-portrait, is a sometime character in the Williams world. Perhaps he arrives with the artist's own tufts of beard, which he could not shave because of his sensitive skin.

At some point in the late 1970s, his compositions reached a level of sophistication and expression that he did not venture beyond until after 1991, the most productive year in his art-making life. His art did not change or broaden, but it deepened. His compositions became denser, with flowers and foliage often nearly obscuring the animals in the background. His ballpoint pen printing of name and date—this begins around 1991—at the bottom front of his drawings declares pride in his work, a pride that all who knew him say he had felt from the start. The larger the public his art found, the more Stuart emphasized that he knew what he was doing. His art moved out of the anonymity of folk art, the precincts of church parish halls, craft fairs, libraries, and the Folkways Café where, had it not been for Mac Doty, it might have remained. As the Currier exhibition demonstrates, Williams was ready to meet the challenge of a wider art world. Through the daunting upheavals in his life, he persisted in his art because he knew that he was "a special person" and that through his art he could communicate his vision of the world.

The wonder is that his wonder at the world and his need to express it never left him. Nor did his art ever lose its sense of humor. Prader-Willi, which imposed so many limits on his life, protected him from the artist's need to speak for his art. In Stuart's world it is all practice and no theory. A red-wheelbarrow-and-white-chickens sort of artist, Stuart knew instinctively that to depict the animals and natural world he most cared for would suffice, for on them, as in William Carlos Williams's famous barnyard scene, "so much depends."

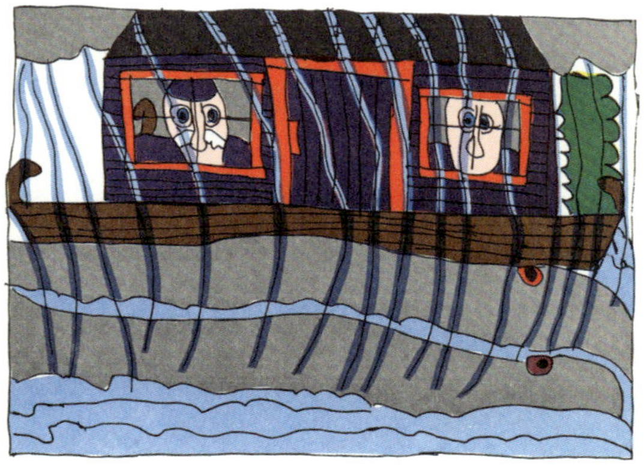
January

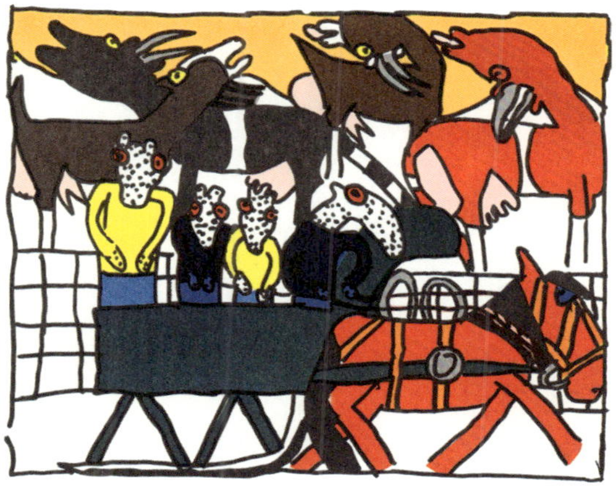
February

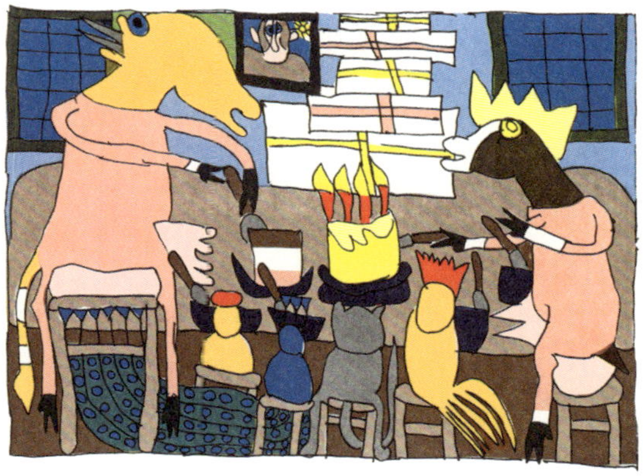
March

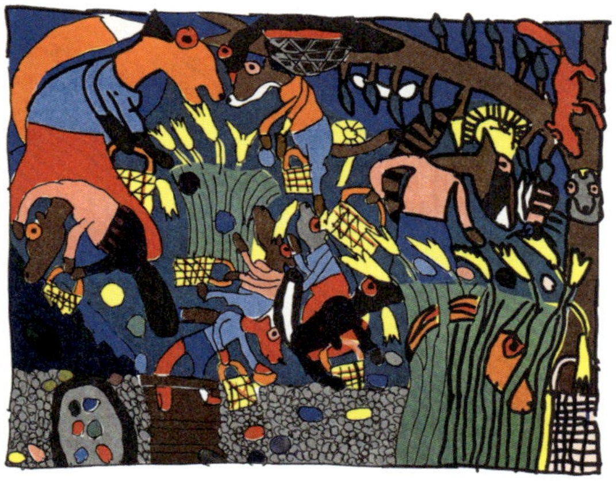
April

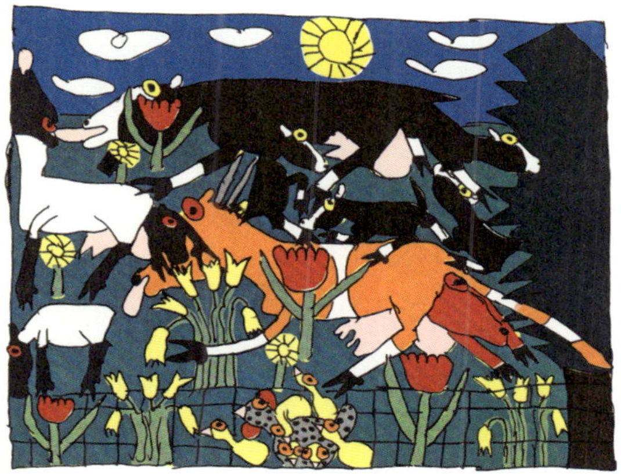
May

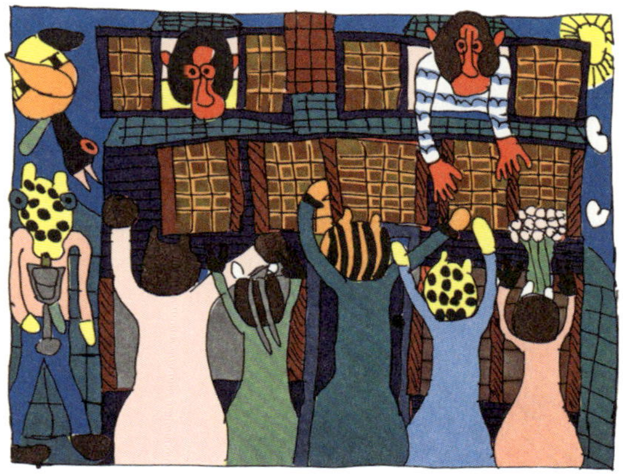
June

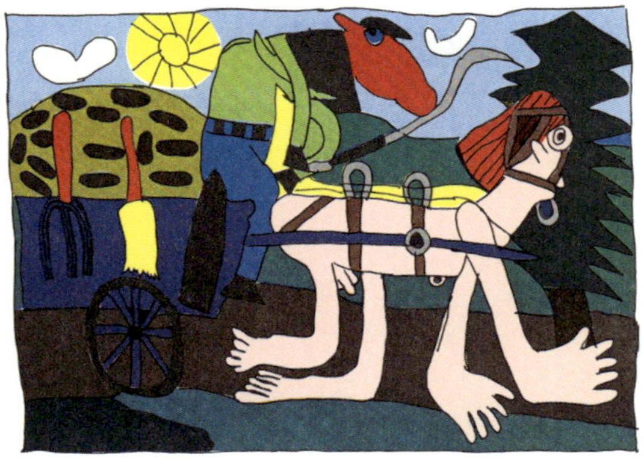
July

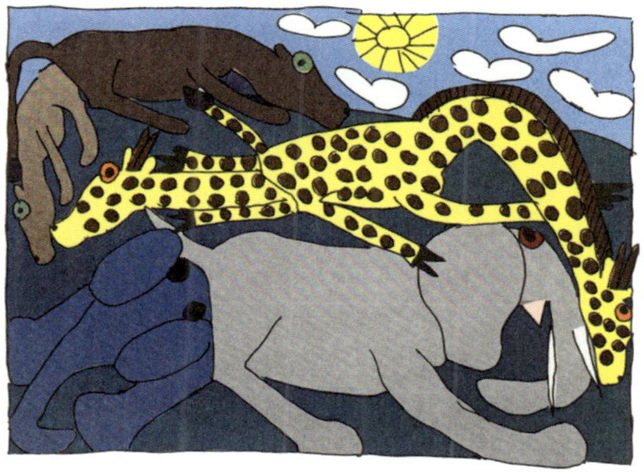
August

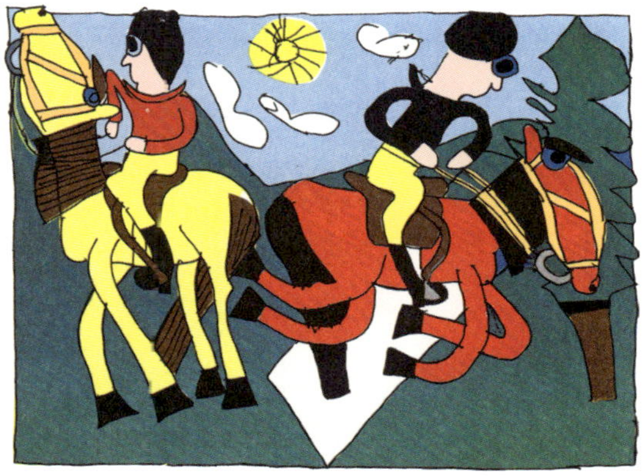
September

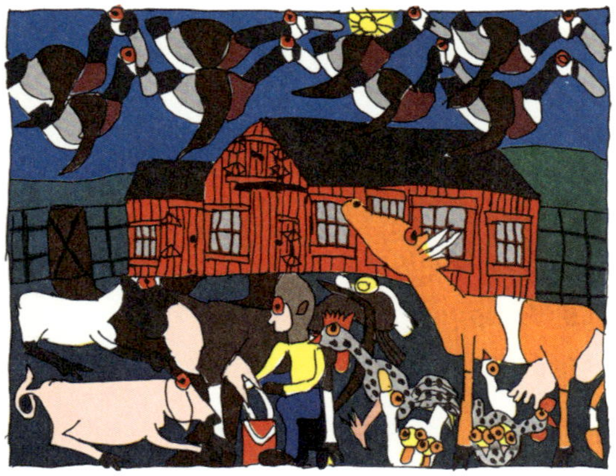
October

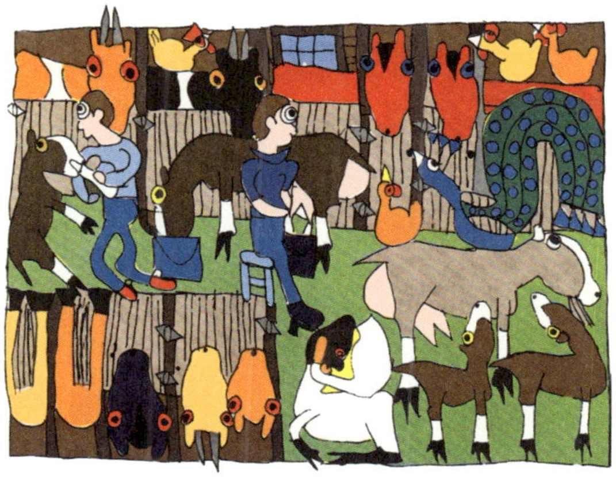
November

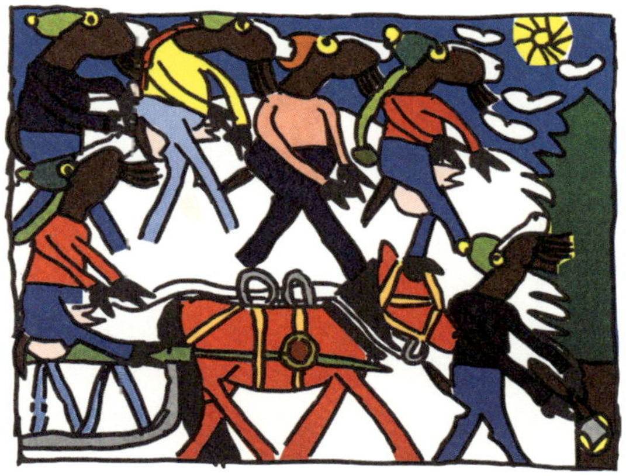
December

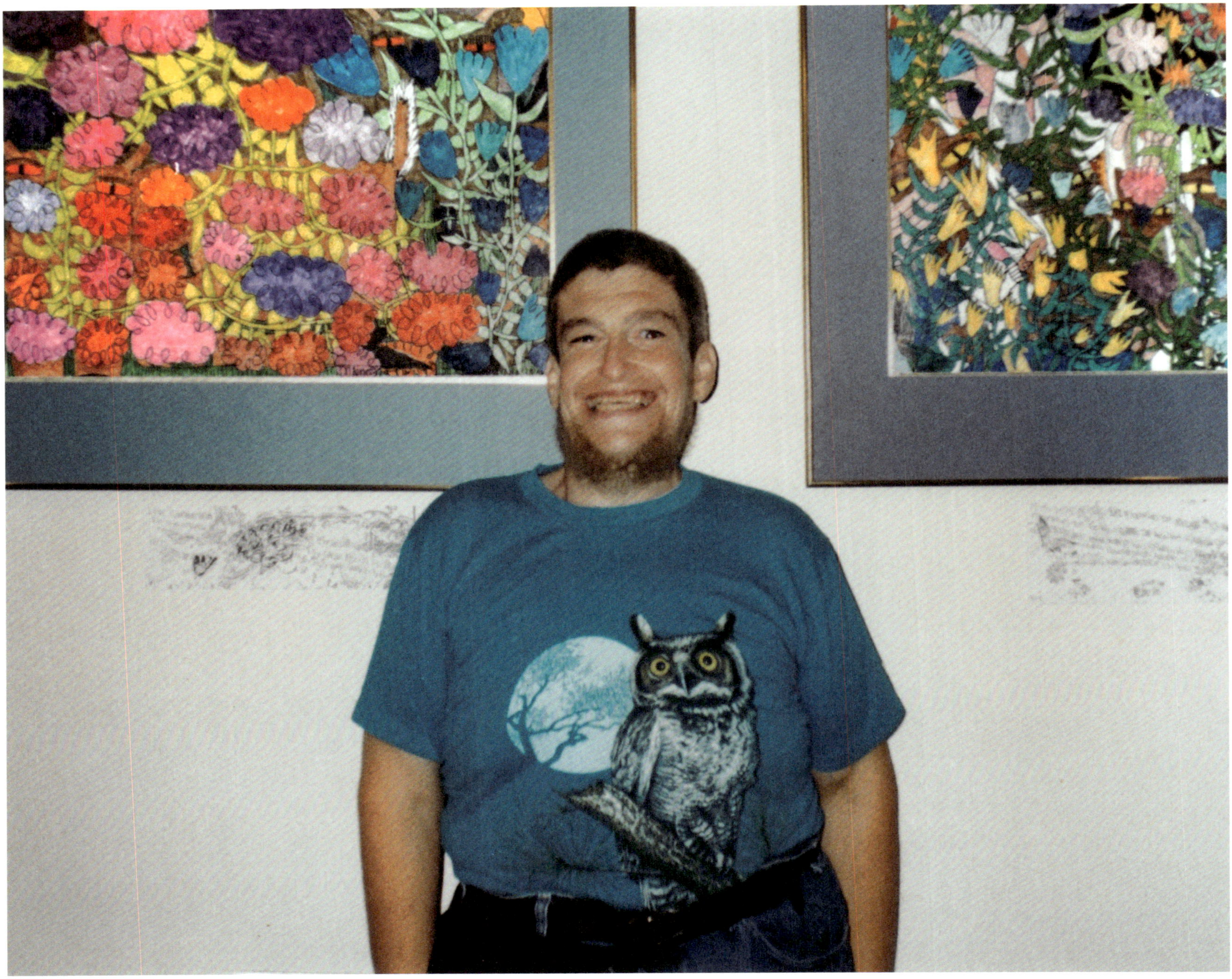

Stuart stands between two of his works at his solo exhibition at the Civic Center in Jaffrey, New Hampshire. The smudges on the wall to either side of him are the captions that he frequently wrote on the back of his pictures.

Prader–Willi Syndrome

When I was introduced to Stuart's art, I had never heard of Prader–Willi. During my years spent researching and writing this book, no one I have spoken to outside of Stuart's family, friends, and the gallery owners who showed his work had heard of the disorder. The rarity of Prader–Willi—1 in 10,000 to 1 in 25,000 newborns—helps account for this. Another factor may be that, at least in the United States for the past two or three generations, most of those with Prader–Willi have lived out of sight, in residential care units. Few of us are likely to encounter someone afflicted with the syndrome.

By displaying wall texts describing Prader–Willi at his Nielsen Gallery and Davis & Langdale Company shows, Stuart meant to educate the public. It is conjecture, but he also may have hoped viewers would ask themselves how one so afflicted could make such art. He never felt that he was typical; nor did the Prader–Willi Syndrome Association think of him as other than extraordinary. As his close friend John Eisenman heard him say many times, Stuart wanted the world to know about Prader–Willi *and* to know he was exceptional as a man and artist.

At Stuart's birth Prader–Willi was without a name. Six years later the disorder, described by doctors Andrea Prader and Heinrich Willi with assistance from other doctors and researchers, had been identified and entered into medical textbooks. Stuart's parents and his Peterborough doctors recognized that Stuart was not typical, but into the 1970s, Prader–Willi was not generally known even within the medical profession. His sister Mary's chance reading of a newspaper article when Stuart was in his twenties brought the news to the Williams family. By then his obsession with food, his physical deformities, his moods and tantrums—all major features of the disorder—were pronounced. But such was his luck and the hard work he put into his art that Prader–Willi did not define Stuart Williams the man or the artist.

Until Stuart reached his mid-thirties, the family had scant knowledge to help them understand and care for him. In his thirty-fifth year, 1985, the Prader–Willi Syndrome Association was formed and published its first newsletter, but clinical studies of the disorder were few before the early 1990s. The Williams family had to depend on observation, instinct, and good fortune in living with Stuart. It is remarkable how well they did.

Studies show that those with Prader–Willi crave routine. Sydney and Mary Williams worked at home, thus providing Stuart with a measure of that. Sydney's putting Stuart in charge of the family goats added a layer of daily order. The luck of living in a small town kept Stuart in the same school for the fourteen years of his education. Sydney's early death did not change this dynamic. Mary continued to work at home on her sculpture and with her horses and riding students. The daily rhythm in the Williams home remained that of farm life.

When Mary realized that Stuart, in his craving for food, had emptied the refrigerator, she padlocked it and the kitchen cupboards. All Prader–Willi literature urges this action to manage the disorder and make possible a lifespan that can, as Stuart's did, extend into the sixties. This will not curb the food obsession, nor will it lessen the high levels of anxiety common to those with Prader–Willi. Tantrums and fights will follow, but without padlocks and diets, obesity and attendant health issues like diabetes will make living difficult and early death likely.

When Mary died, Stuart's siblings, leading their own lives and never having prepared a plan for Stuart's care, had no substitute for her. Their understanding of Prader–Willi, absent the Internet and before the studies available now, was spotty at best. His mother's death, on his birthday, triggered memories of his father's death on the same date, intensifying his grief and contributing to his severe depression. Stuart entered into a period of hospitalizations and, for the first time, antipsychotic drugs. Gradually, stability returned, but as Stuart aged, all of Prader–Willi's prominent symptoms claimed him. The overeating, obsessions, stubbornness, tantrums, anxiety, and sadness typical of the disorder characterized his behavior. No one outgrows Prader–Willi.

Recent studies of those with Prader–Willi have explored the differences between those categorized as "active and extroverted toddlers" and those as "passive and introvert." This layman's reading of the literature, and what Stuart's siblings remember of his toddler years, places Stuart in both categories but with more tendencies toward extroversion. It is not easy to say how this prefigured his future. An observation that may be applicable to Stuart when he was older compared adults with Prader–Willi to adults with other intellectual disabilities; those with Prader–Willi are "prone to . . . repetitive, compulsive-like behaviors such as hoarding, ordering and arranging." This does fit Stuart, although Pablo Picasso, Andy Warhol, and a host of other artists not afflicted with Prader–Willi could also be so described.

For all that Prader–Willi limited Stuart, it relieved him of the constraints of a conventional education. Typical children do not spend fourteen years in the same school, free of grades and promotion, drawing as they please. When children learn how to read, most begin to abandon drawing as a form of communication. This did not happen to Stuart—perhaps because by the time he became a reader, drawing was ingrained in him.

In his life as an artist, Prader–Willi relieved Stuart of the artist's compulsion to explain and justify himself and his work. After Fleur Weymouth's lesson about overlapping figures ended his frustration with pictorial space, Stuart does not appear to have struggled with his art. No one ever heard him complain about not being able to work or express doubts about the quality of work he had produced. Stuart's pictorial intelligence is manifest throughout his body of work (notwithstanding a test, administered in his forties, that assessed him to have "mild retardation" and which almost certainly did not take into account his art). He was a confident artist and did not, it appears, suffer the doubt that besets so many artists.

Stuart was born not only in the right place but at the right time. Had he been born in, say 1980, after Prader–Willi had been described and treatment established, he may have been placed in a Prader–Willi community. This sort of well-meaning, humane, and effective supervision might inadvertently have stifled whatever gifts he had as an artist. He grew up

Lazy Susan, acrylic on wood.

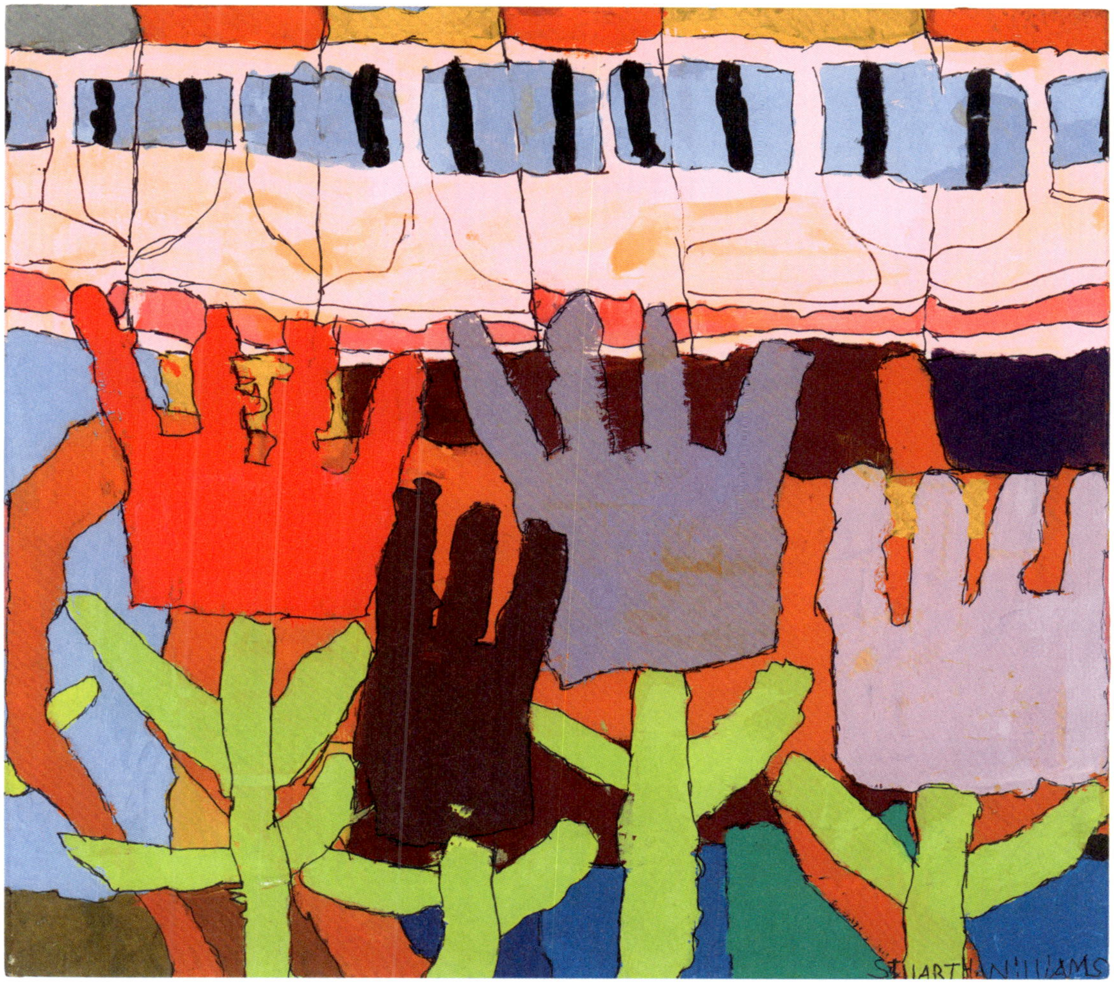

independent of such care, treated more or less like the rest of his siblings. When Stuart learned about these communities, he was adamant that he would never live in one.

Stuart transcended the limits Prader-Willi placed upon him, but neither Stuart's life nor his art can be divorced from Prader-Willi. To take the full measure of his art, it is vital to have some idea of the obstacles Stuart overcame, of the life demands that nearly overwhelmed him. It is also necessary to consider the transformative powers of art. No matter the prison of our lives, the impulse to make something—that deepest of human desires—can set us free to imagine a world. The bees ascendant in Stuart's late work are emblems of the industry he applied to following his imagination into the Edens he created.

After Stuart's death John Eisenman described this vision of his friend in a letter to Stuart's brother Frank: "I imagine Stuart up in Heaven, traveling around in a Red Ferrari, with a beautiful wife, eating in the best restaurants; a Famous artist with an adventurous and Fulfilling Life."

On January 15, 2014, under the headline "Seeking Clues to Obesity in Rare Hunger Disorder" the *New York Times* ran an article on Prader-Willi. The biopharmaceutical company Zafgen is studying the syndrome in the hopes of developing a therapy to treat obesity. The research trial is small, only seventeen people, but results have been encouraging; its drug beloranib has helped Prader-Willi subjects lose weight.

According to the article, the Prader-Willi Syndrome Association knows of at least 8,000 Americans living with the condition. Since so little attention has been paid to the syndrome, the Association is eager to encourage more individuals to participate in the testing. Zafgen's interest can only provide insight into the mysteries surrounding Prader-Willi, and perhaps offer potential benefits for those with the disorder.

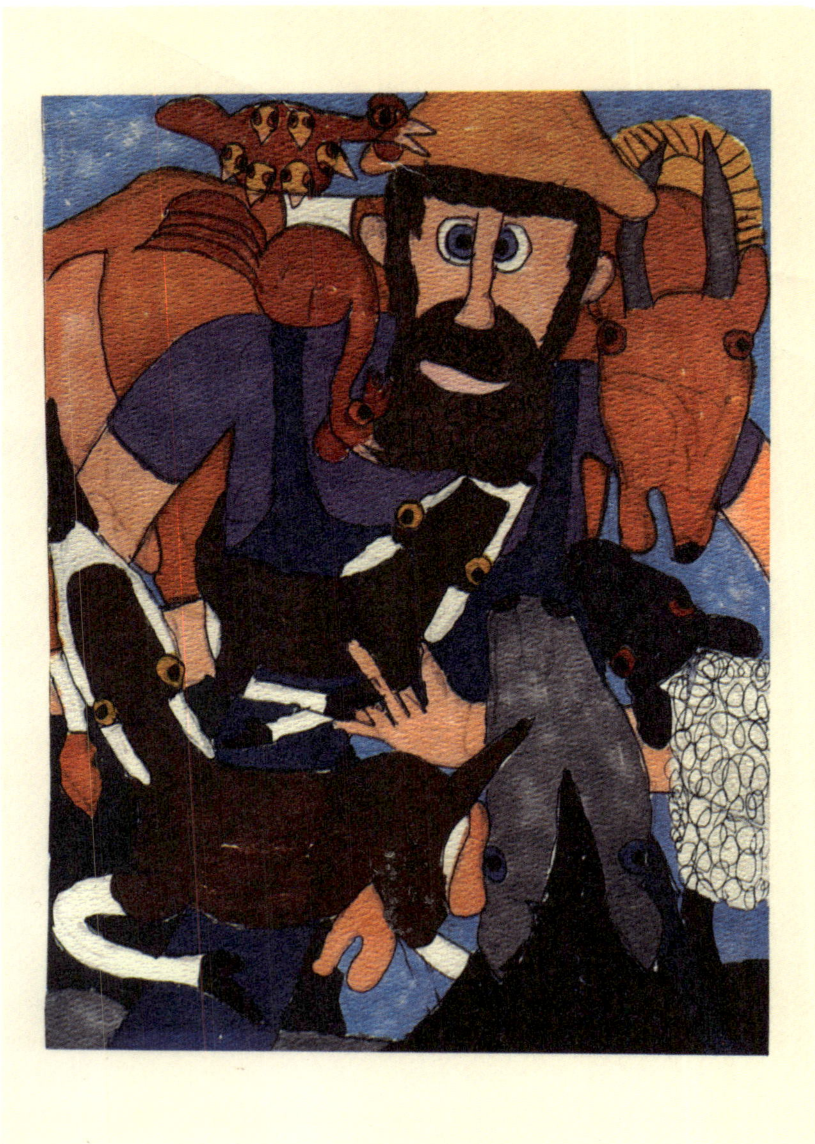

The Farmer And His Friends, one of the four postcards Stuart published under his Creature Prints imprint.

The Farmer's Dream

ADRIENNE JACOBSON

Throughout his forty-five-year artistic career, Stuart Williams focused on animals. By his early twenties, he had drawn the menagerie of creatures that surrounded him every day: the goats, horses, cows, peacocks, barn cats, dogs, and ducks around his family's New Hampshire farm, as well as the local wildlife—deer, foxes, squirrels, birds, fish, and bears. He especially liked to depict bumblebees. After his first trip to Africa, at age twenty-seven, Stuart added lions, elephants, antelope, giraffes, gorillas, and other exotic animals he had seen there. His bold compositions—with their expressive outlines, bright colors, and flat shapes—endow the figures with a weighty presence; they seem to take up more space than their actual area on the page. He emphasized his subjects' eyes and in later work often turned their faces to gaze at the viewer head-on. For Stuart, drawing these animals may have been a way of caring for them. He observed their rituals of birth, feeding, hunting, hiding, and becoming prey. The bright, solid colors and repeated, simplified forms, especially those of the eyes and mouths, give vitality to the creatures in his paper world.

In the years after his mother Mary's death in 1990, when Stuart was forty, his art gradually took a new turn. He began to hide animals behind increasingly dense screens of foliage. Why, when clarity and graphic simplicity are paramount in Stuart's early work, did he begin to overlap his shapes to the point of almost totally obscuring his subjects? Was it an experiment in space and composition? If so, why did this become prevalent in the 1990s? And why did he begin to give these animals a voice by having them speak short first-person narratives he hand-lettered on the backs of many of these drawings?

Many of the circumstances that shaped Stuart's life and art can be traced to his being born with Prader-Willi syndrome, a rare genetic disorder that affects appetite, muscle control, physical appearance, and development and learning. Until she died, his mother remained his primary caregiver, tending to his daily routine. She gave him support, security, and stability, yet in her efforts to manage the uncontrollable hunger that is the hallmark of Prader-Willi, her strict control over his diet and food intake also made her the focus of his deep frustration. Her death took away not only the person who knew Stuart and his needs best but also his childhood home; eventually, he would find himself in a series of assisted-living placements. Despite attempts by his brothers and sisters to help him, Stuart fell into a deep depression that required several hospitalizations. He dealt with his grief by devoting himself to his art, but he was often angry and felt overlooked and unheard by his family.

It was around this time that he began superimposing rhythmic patterns of foliage, weather, or water over the figures of his subjects. Perhaps he was expressing his sorrow and resentment by hiding them in his art as he felt himself hidden from and misunderstood by the world. Or perhaps the environments surrounding them had gained a new importance for him. Their voices, captured in the narratives on the back of many of these images, suggest that the animals are facing hunger or fearful of predators. In the books he read and the nature programs that he watched on television, Stuart must have sensed the danger the modern world had brought to his beloved animals and their habitats.

According to his older brother Frank, Stuart declared his intention to be an artist before he reached his teens. Their parents were both artists, and he began his formal art education at the nearby Sharon Art Center when he was thirteen. At various local venues, Stuart sold his art while still a teenager. By the age of twenty-two, he had an outlet for his postcards and calendars at his brother Willard's Toadstool Bookstore in Peterborough. Stuart's early work shows clearly articulated animal forms spread across the picture plane. His talent for color and composition moves the viewer's eye around each scene in a playful loop. An undated, probably circa 1970–76, farm scene exemplifies Stuart's early artistic method [Plate 30]. At first glance, the animals seem to be flying over a red barn. A closer look reveals that they are situated on a hillside above the barn and that each is giving birth. The laboring livestock fill every inch of the picture plane in an irregular design. Each shape is saturated in one flat color, with minimal color mixing. Visible marker strokes give the scene texture.

None of the lines in the drawing are ruler-straight, from the slightly askew barn windows to the animals' bent limbs and limp, extended tongues. Perhaps the cast-rubber toys his parents produced during his childhood for their Red Shed Rubber Toy line influenced Stuart's elastic representation of his subjects. He would use the same shapes again and again, until they became an integral part of his pictorial vocabulary.

Stuart's repeated shapes and patterns serve to unify his compositions. This method emphasizes the emotional content of the scene and often connects the emotions of humans and animals. When Stuart was six years old, his father gave him the responsibility of caring for the farm's goats; he based the image of a goat nursing her kid in *Untitled (The wild mountain top flowers are blooming in their wild glory)* (1992) on his years of close observation of his charges. The work balances dark brown curves at the top and bottom, creating a frame for the drawing [Plate 9]. Sometime in the 1970s or early 1980s, Stuart wrote and illustrated a 273-page book chronicling his experiences with his small herd. In one sequence of ten drawings, *Gisela Eating My Sketch Pad,* Stuart is contentedly drawing one of his goats [see pages 27–36]. The goat approaches and begins eating his paper. She consumes the entire sketchbook. Stuart then cries a flurry of amoeba-shaped tears. Gisela returns to Stuart to comfort him. This portrait playfully merges Stuart's two identities: goatherd and artist.

Throughout his career Stuart's iconography maintained remarkable uniformity. Like Egyptian hieroglyphs, Stuart's forms achieved a concise legibility. His sheep, goats, donkeys, horses, cows, peacocks, and hens retain the same appearance over years and decades. His method of representing a sun always involves a circle and surrounding rays, with the entire area colored yellow: suns from his 1976 calendar are almost identical to those he made twenty years later. Stuart's strategy for drawing eyes, stars, bees, and flowers are similarly standardized. His bees are particularly stylized, with their rectangular, striped bodies, round eyes, and blue wings. (In a rare example of change in his visual vocabulary, in the 1970s he always depicted eyes as round—giving his figures a look of constant surprise; between the 1980s and the 1990s, however, Stuart began to use oval-shaped eyes for all creatures except birds.)

In *Untitled (We are three hungry foxes on the prowl)* [Plate 14], a trio of similarly drawn foxes give the picture rhythm and movement as they circle a hilltop. Details like a flower, a sun, and featherlike wheat stalks move the gaze around the hill, as the viewer visually performs the same dance that the foxes enact.

While many of Stuart's shapes remained uniform, the relationship of the animals to the viewers changed. Before the 1990s, many of Stuart's figures are in profile. But by the mid-1990s, he was emphasizing the subject's outward gaze. Comparing two winter farm scenes shows this evolution. In a drawing made sometime in the 1980s, cows, goats, and horses move through the snow [Plate 32]. They are engrossed in the action; none of their faces are turned to look out at the viewer. A second winter image, from a later but uncertain date, portrays all of the animals looking out of the picture plane [Plate 21]. A horse and a dog twist their heads toward us as they jump in synchrony, as if performing for the viewer. The bright purple sleigh behind them lifts dangerously. Even the horses in the barn peer out the window toward us. The two humans look on, seemingly surprised at what they are witnessing.

Two scenes of African safaris further highlight the animal gaze [Plates 12 and 13]. Stuart went on safari twice—once in 1977 and again in 1986. These drawings were probably made between 1986 and 1990. Before the 1990s, many of Stuart's figures are in profile. But by the mid-1990s, he was emphasizing the subject's outward gaze. In both, the animals' round eyes stare back at the viewer with surprise and anticipation, as though waiting for us to intervene in some way and wondering what action we will take. There is minimal overlap between the figures and the environment. The human faces in the first look at a cheetah chasing an antelope. The people are the ones in captivity, confined behind the van window. In the second drawing, lions twist their faces to get a good view of the safari van. They observe it curiously while the humans stare ahead in profile. The animals seem to examine and judge the tourists, who are again in a cage of their own.

When they do appear, men and women are never depicted on their own; they are always interacting with or watching animals. One of Stuart's favorite motifs was the benevolent farmer hugging his charges close, the man's rubberlike arms stretching around a dense knot of figures. In a drawing made in all likelihood post-1990, a dark-skinned farmer holds a group including a sheep, a horse, a donkey, a goat, a chicken, ducks, and other livestock. He has almond-shaped eyes—a characteristic of those with Prader-Willi—and a satisfied smile, while the beasts gaze at the viewer with rounded, surprised eyes. In another picture, a naked, kissing couple embrace sheep, goats, horses, and ducks. Although the humans' genitals are exposed, the composition focuses on their kiss and the surrounding biting, licking mouths. The creatures' jaws are open, soundlessly calling out in ecstasy. Yet their euphoria seems to be that of a dog who sees his master returning, rather than erotic desire. The man and woman press their mouths together but hold their nude bodies apart, encom-

Robin Eating Nightcrawler, marker, ink, and pencil on paper, n.d. Stuart exploring the theme of animals hiding in plain sight so as to better observe humans.

passing the animals in a collective embrace of familial, not coital, love.

As his style matured, Stuart increased the density and layers in his compositions until they began to mask his subjects. These later drawings focus on the creatures' habitats, portrayed in repeated geometric shapes and colors, and winding foliage. From the 1990s until his death in 2012, Stuart drew scrims that he layered on top of his subjects like lattices. Similar to those used in theater, these scrims are flat, and often but not always obscure what is behind them. The result is a thick and rhythmic composition that hides the animal in the background. In *Untitled (It is a beautiful spring day here in Milford, N.H.)* from 1994 [Plate 11], a bird is clearly visible through spreading branches. Two pairs of human eyes looking through the windows of a house in the background are harder to discern. This composition compresses four layers—foliage, bird, building, and human figures—into one two-dimensional picture plane. The variety of screens that Stuart came to employ illustrates his incredible range, planning, and detail. The red-breasted bird (identified in the inscription as a bluebird) is completely enmeshed in gray boughs punctuated with green leaf buds. The orange house with its wooden siding has screened windows edged in muted blue-green. Behind one screen, a set of enormous rectangular blue eyes with brown lashes occupies the top right of the image, while the red-lashed eye of a second person peeks out from the bottom right.

Even when the viewer cannot visually identify the creature, Stuart made their presence clear in the vignette-like captions that he wrote to accompany his images. Written from the point of view of the animal, they detail important aspects of the habitat, including weather, predators, and possible food sources. The narrative for *Untitled (It is a beautiful spring day here in Milford, N.H.)* reinforces the scene's complexity, with details that might otherwise go unnoticed by human eyes: It is spring and, as the viewer can see if she looks closely, the "leaves on the oak tree are budding." The bluebird says, "I have some wild bird seed in my beak from bird feeder hanging in maple tree." A single tan seed balances in its beak. Stuart's inscription describes the two people in the background, one getting ready for work and the other making breakfast. It ends by drawing attention to the flowers blooming in Mrs. Johnston's garden, two of which can be seen in the bottom left corner. Like his bold graphic style, these written narratives actualize the animals' existence, bringing their needs and experiences to the foreground.

Frequently, Stuart's narratives recycle the same language, the textual equivalent of his repeated graphic motifs. The sun—always shown as a golden orb emanating straight rays—is usually shining, and the wildflowers are blooming (triangular tulips or open flowers with loops to signify petals). A typical caption will begin or end with, "It is a beautiful spring day," or "The wild mountain-top flowers are blooming." On the back of an image depicting a woodpecker in a sugar maple [Plate 17], Stuart wrote,

> The maple tree leaves are slowing budding in this old maple tree, is slowly dying from hole that the reddy The red headed wood pecker has been here(?). ~~There are four purple flowers~~. If I espace

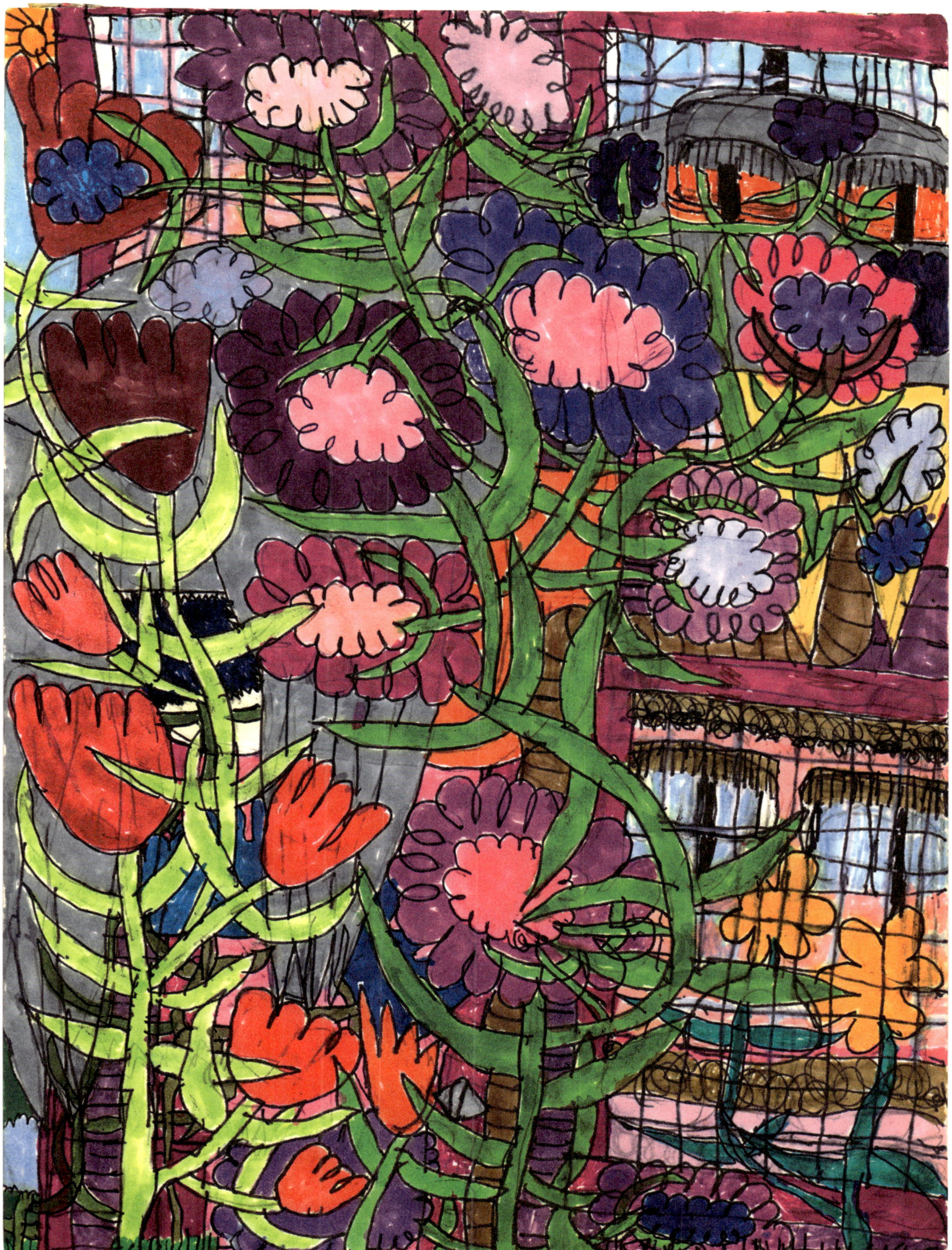

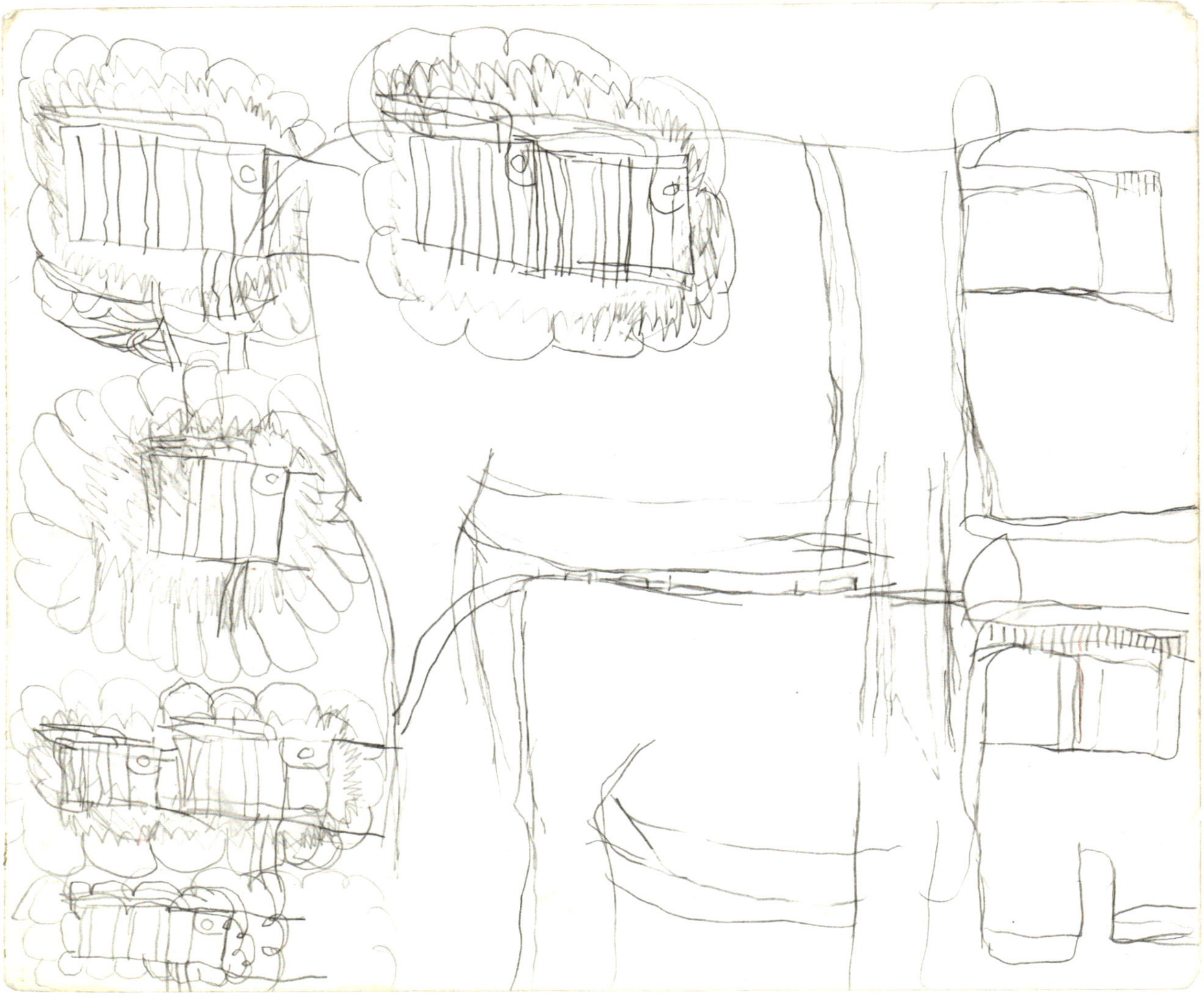

by going up the tree trunk, I will not be eaten also. There are four purple wild flowers blooming.

Sometimes the animal is so obscured by flowers, branches, or water that it is all but imperceptible. Only the mouth and eyes, the parts of the body that Stuart emphasized most, remain discernable. One particularly dense late work seems to be a bright image of bees and flowers, sliding along the color spectrum from violet on the left to orange, red, yellow, and blue on the right [Plate 1]. Thin black pen lines zip through the images, like the trails of flying bees. Shapes and colors cover the entirety of the picture plane.

In the last decade of his career, Stuart assimilated exotic creatures—such as the camels that are the (almost totally obscured) subject of this image—into floral surroundings. The viewer can barely see the camels' open mouths with white teeth and pink tongues bent to the ground, grazing; there might be some humps at the top of the image, but the flowers and bees completely mask most of the camels. Stuart's last exhibition during his lifetime, in 2006 at the Davis & Langdale Company gallery in New York, displayed at least ten similar layered compositions, with bees and blossoms covering each drawing's subject.

Stuart's unfinished drawings give insight into how he achieved this daunting intricacy. In one graphite sketch of two bovine animals, he is just beginning to superimpose rectangular bees sitting on flowers over the hefty mammals. In his completed pictures, the flowers are connected by a web of stems, but here we can see how he drew the animal almost completely before layering imagery over it. Stuart's next step was to go over the pencil with black ink. A thickly layered drawing of a mule deer shows a latter step in his process: bees and flowers cover the foreground, interrupted only by a cactus; in the background, the eyelashes of the mule deer are barely visible. Stuart always left the eyes exposed, perhaps to fix the viewer in their stare. To finish his pictures, he colored in his

At his death Stuart left pads and portfolios of undated drawings. These pencil drawings show him using variations on the grid that Fleur Weymouth introduced him to in his youth.

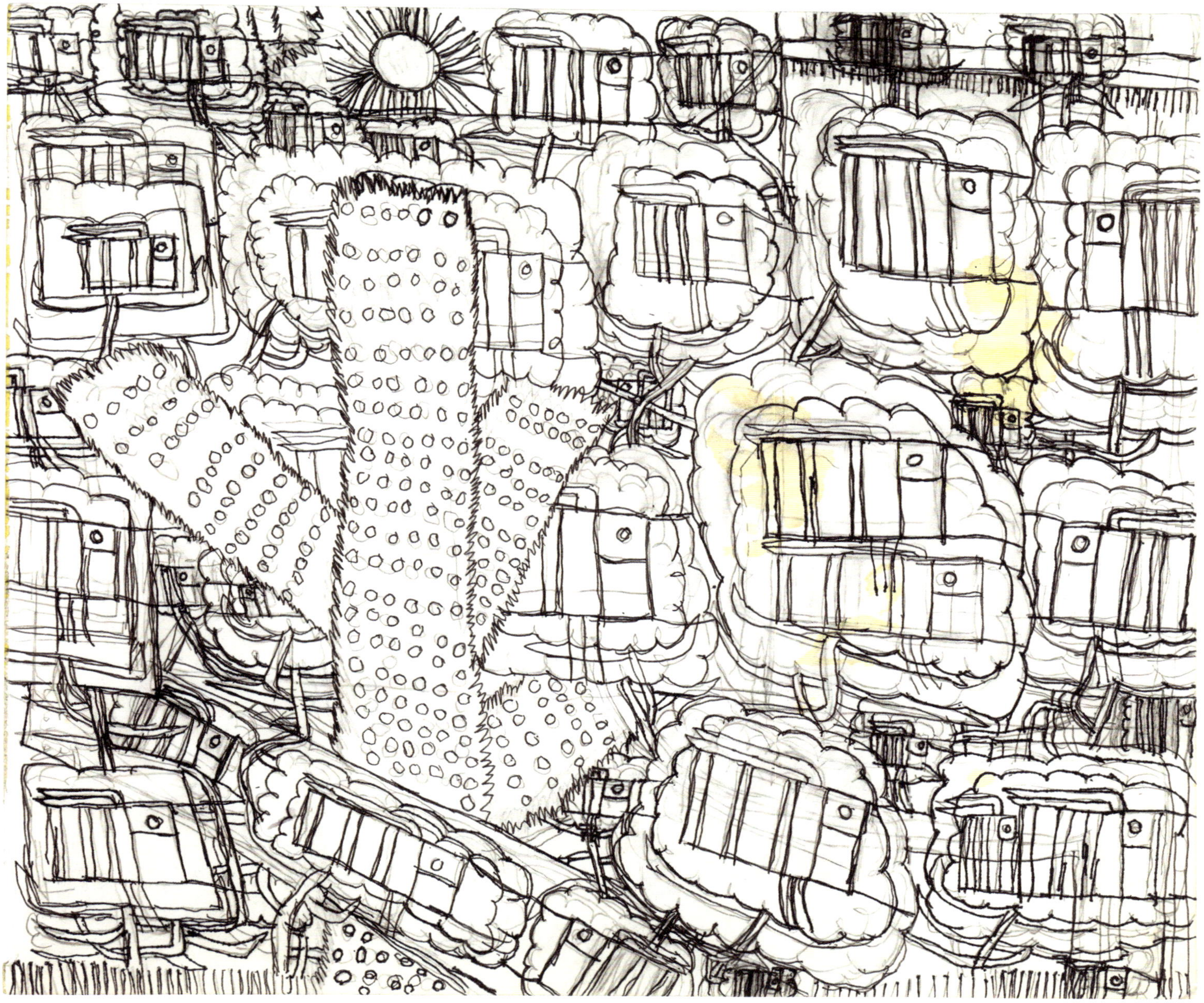

shapes, giving them the well-defined, concrete presence that is a hallmark of his art.[1]

Whatever their purpose might have been for Stuart, the scrims represent the wildlife habitat, which Stuart knew to be increasingly fragile, daily threatened, and rapidly diminishing. The animals appear to be in yet another cage of human making. They look out, forlorn and perhaps accusingly; they plead—all states of mind well known by Stuart after a lifetime of feeling himself to be never completely seen.

1. Other works where the animal is masked include *Untitled (It is a hot warm day here in Nelson N.H. on Center Pond)* (hiding a moose) [Plate 3], *Untitled (It is a spring day on the African Plain here in Tanzania)* (two elephants) [Plate 7], and *Untitled (It's midnight and it is snowing hard)* (a snowy owl) [Plate 2].

According to his family, Stuart hoped to be an ambassador for animals, advocating for their rights and depicting the facts of their world. All who know his pictures will agree with *Boston Globe* art critic Sebastian Smee that "each of his drawings suggests an enviably deep, somehow magical identification with [animals]."[2] In his image of a man embracing two black bears [Plate 4], the animals' teeth and eyes are clearly visible, while the human is partially hidden behind both mugging beasts, pushing them forward Could this have been Stuart's wish, that humans show empathy to their fellow creatures and put animals first for the good of all?

2. "Taking the Pulse of 'Art as Healing' at the Danforth," *Boston Globe,* March 29 2014.

Plates

1 Untitled (We are called Bactrian Camels by two legged people)

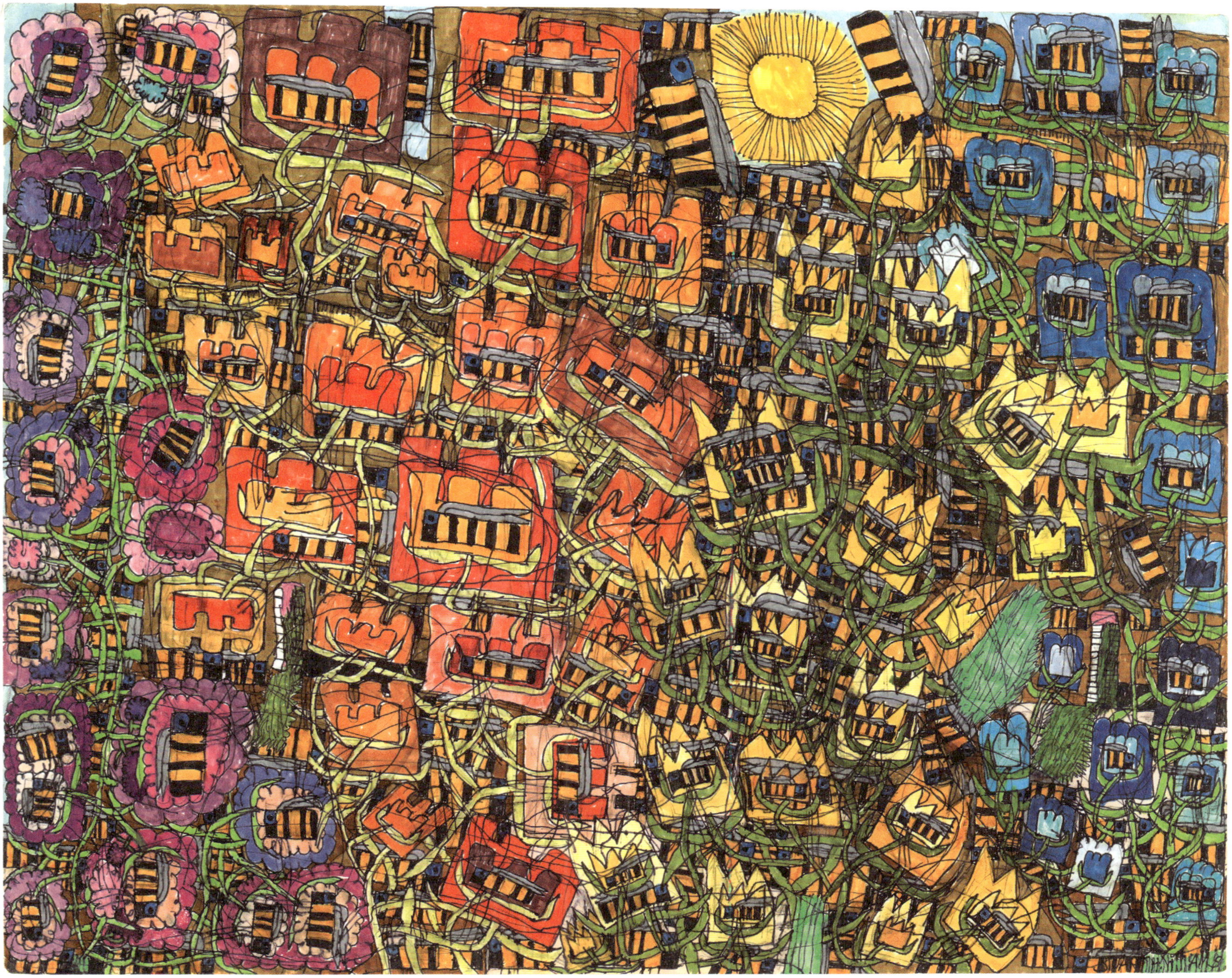

2 Untitled (It's midnight and it is snowing hard)

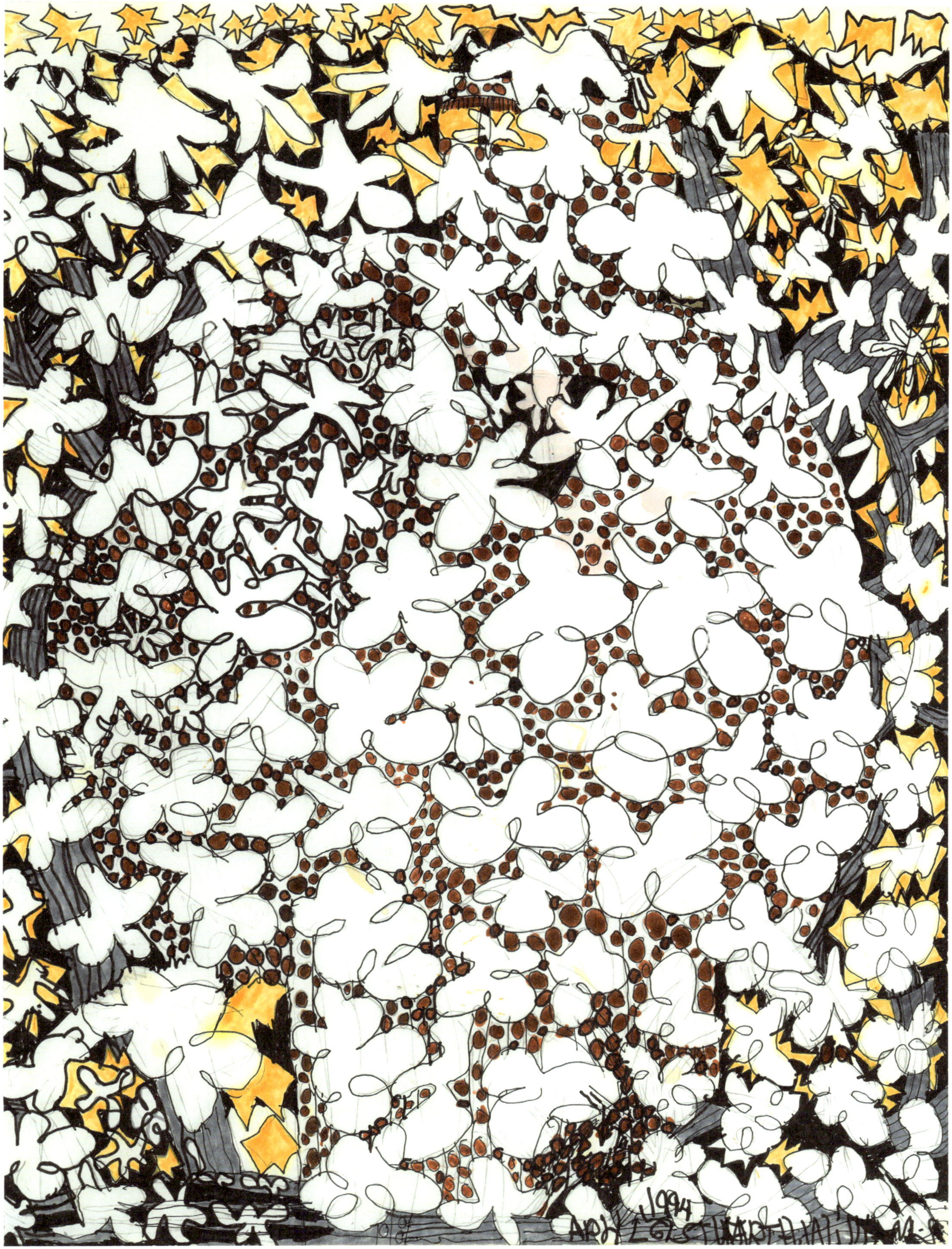

3 Untitled (It is a hot warm day here in Nelson N.H. on Center Pond)

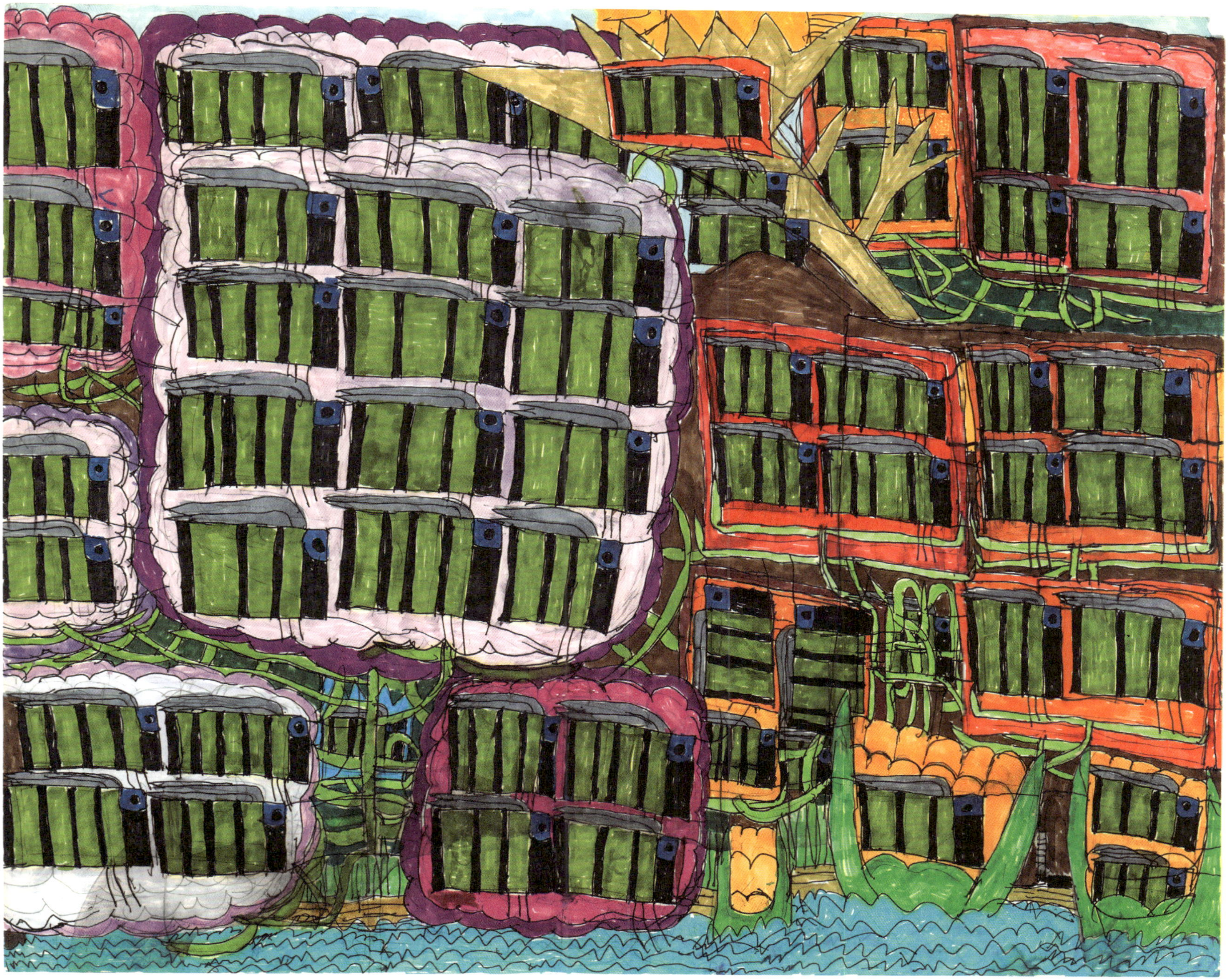

4 Untitled (My friend the black bears, there I raise two from cubs)

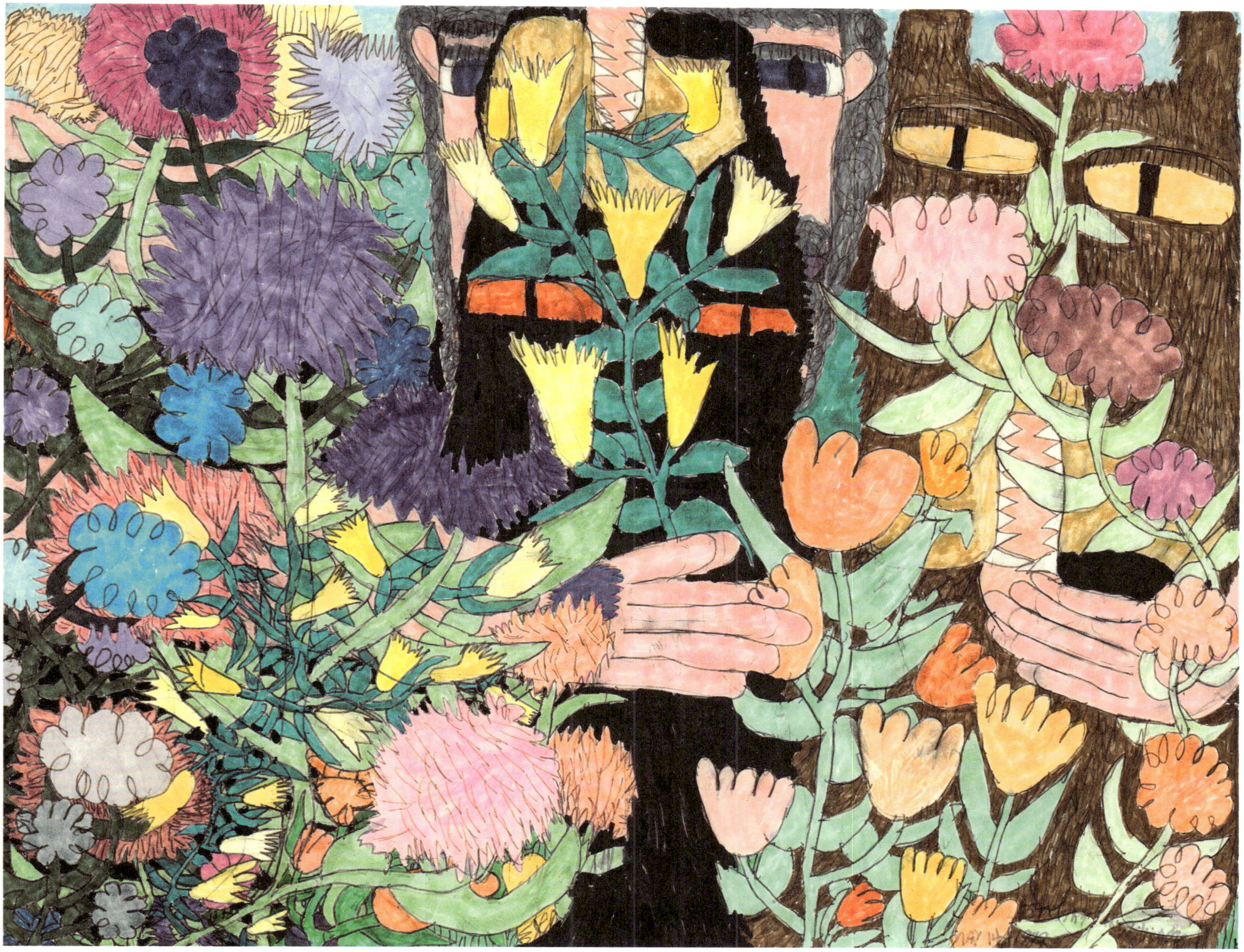

5 2 Ostriches

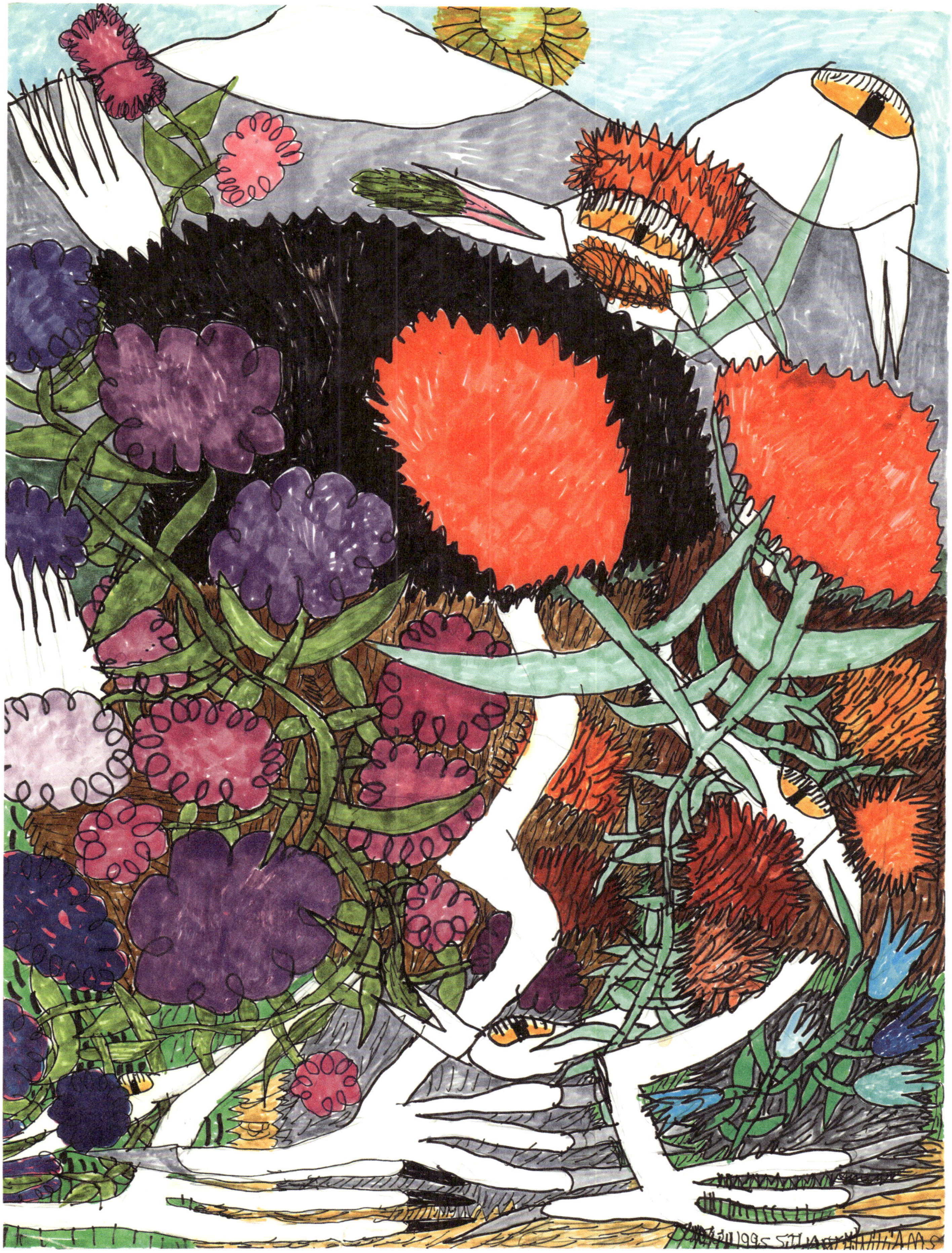

6 Untitled (Honk, Honk my mate and I are coming into land on Jagger Pond)

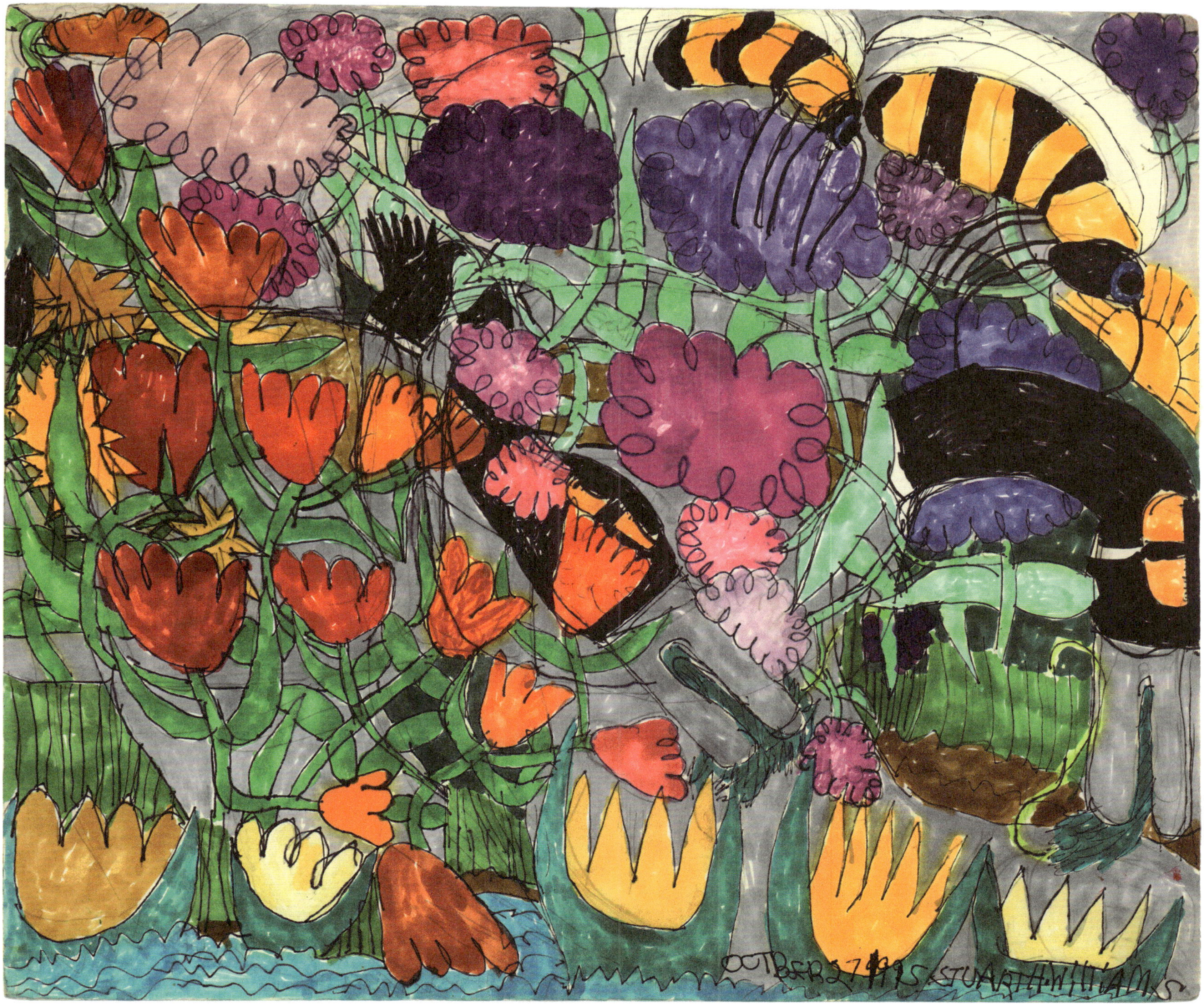
OOTBER 27 1995 STUART.H.WILLIAMS

7 Untitled (It is a spring day on the African Plain here in Tanzania)

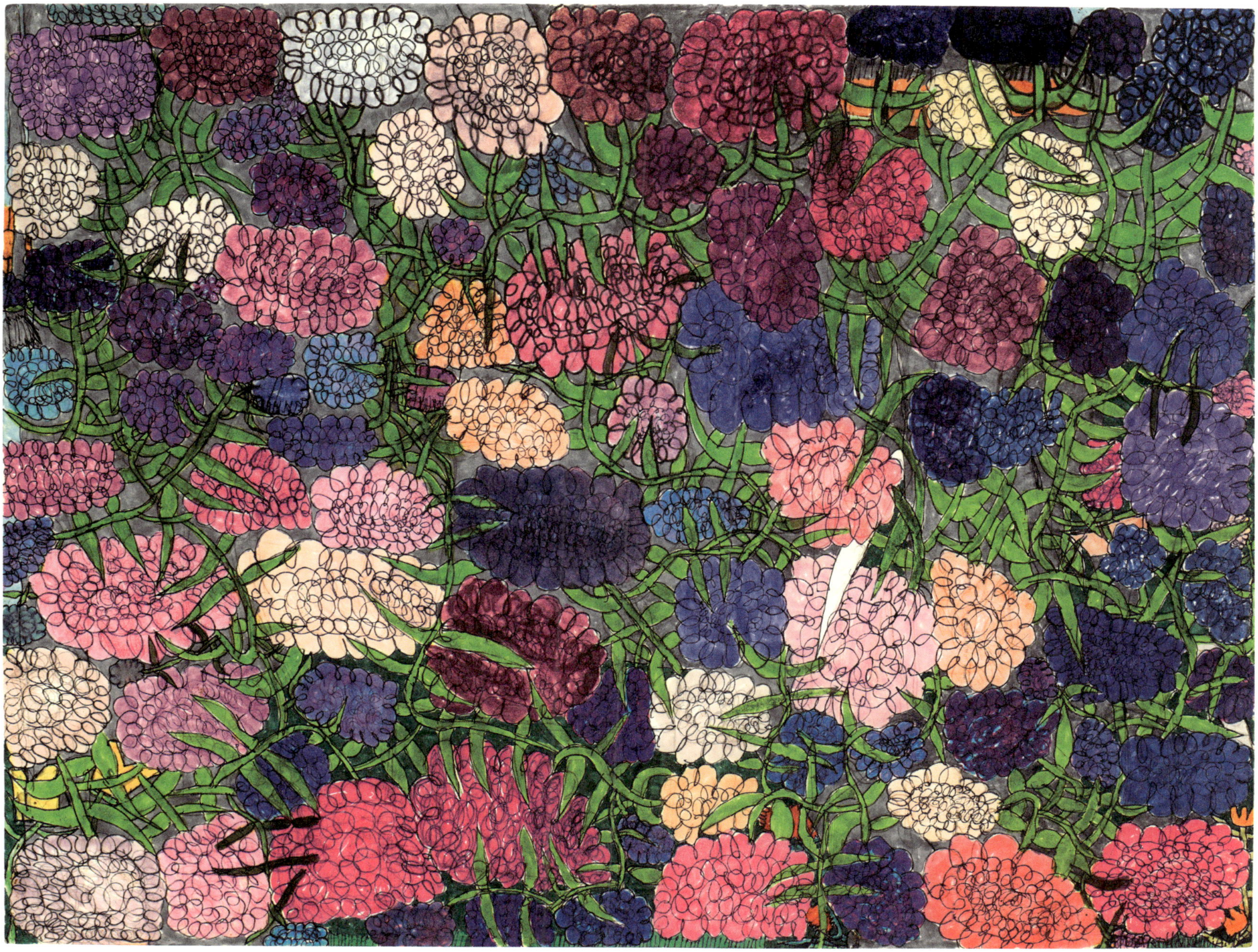

8 Untitled (The red clown fish has me in his jaw and eating darn)

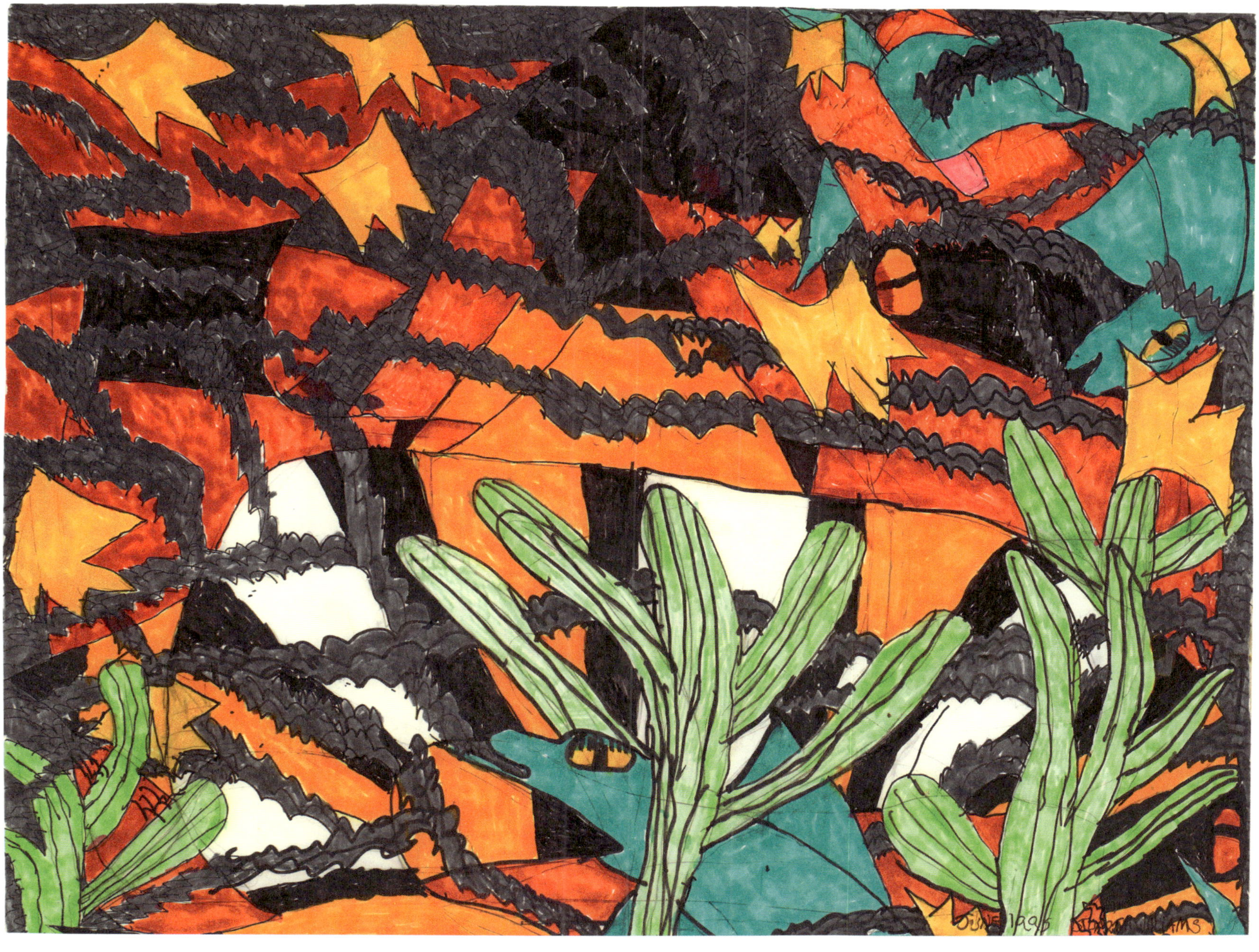

9 Untitled (The wild mountain top flowers are blooming in their wild glory)

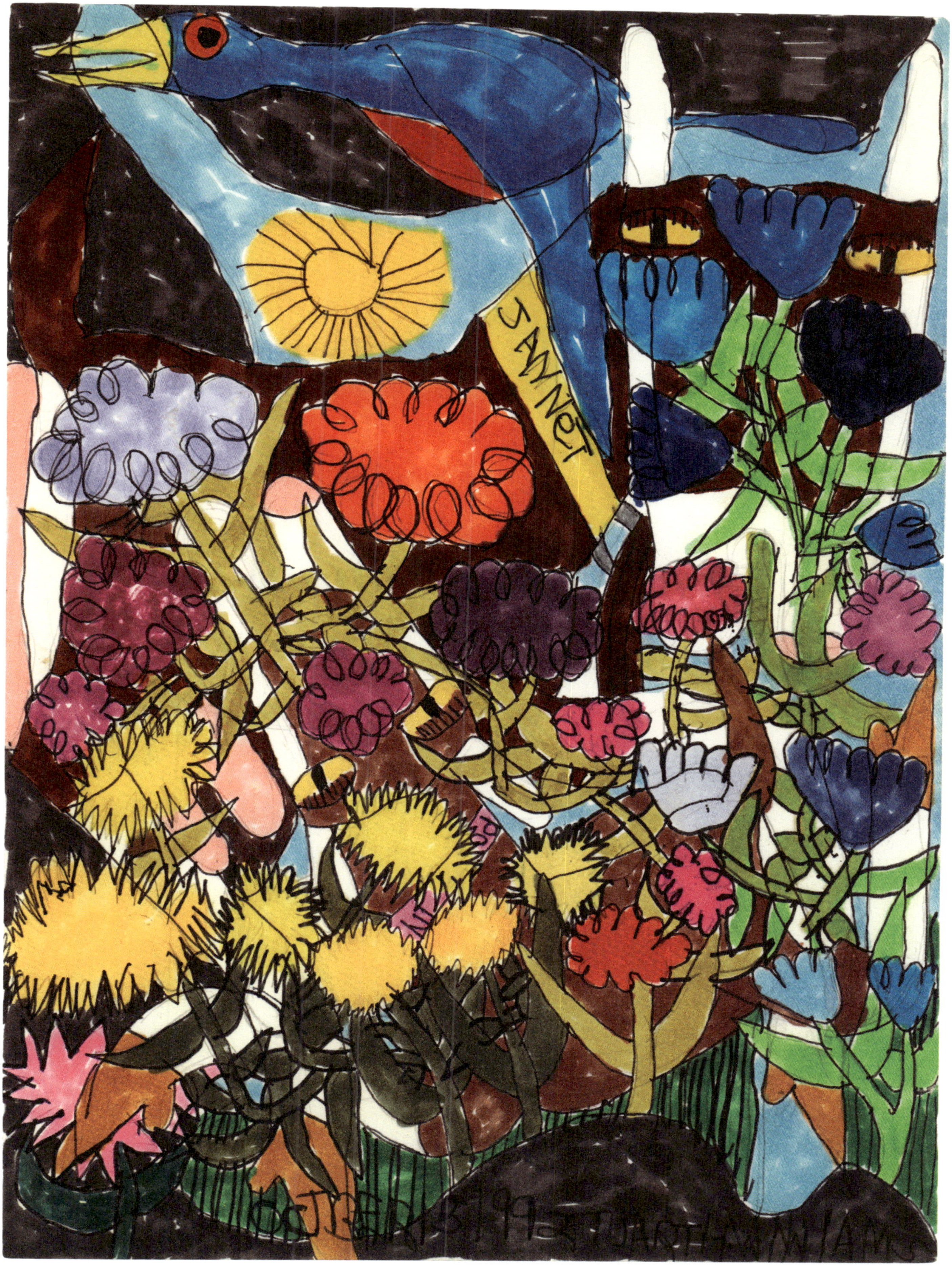
JANNOT

10 Untitled (The warm of the sun feel good on my back)

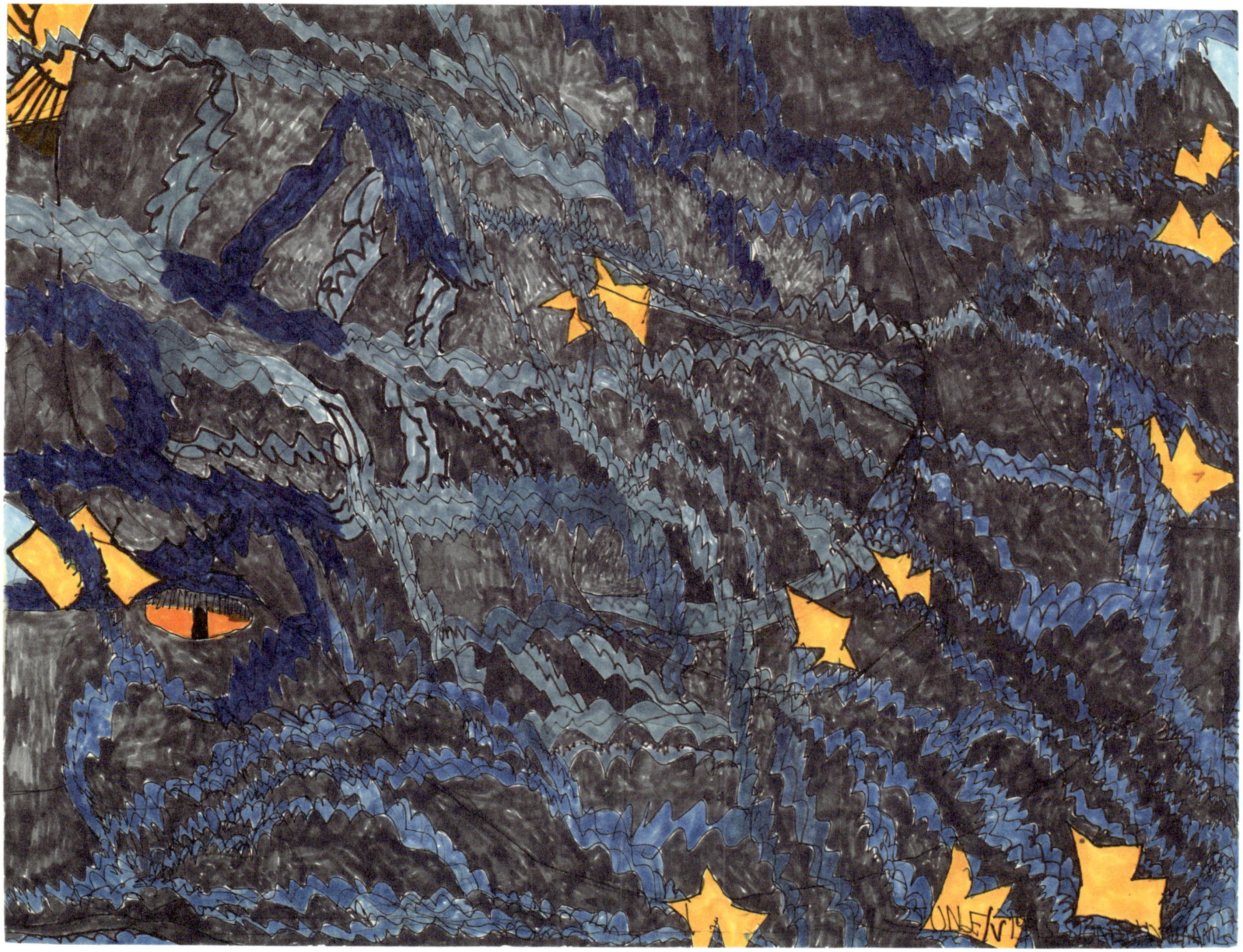

11 Untitled (It is a beautiful spring day here in Milford, N.H.)

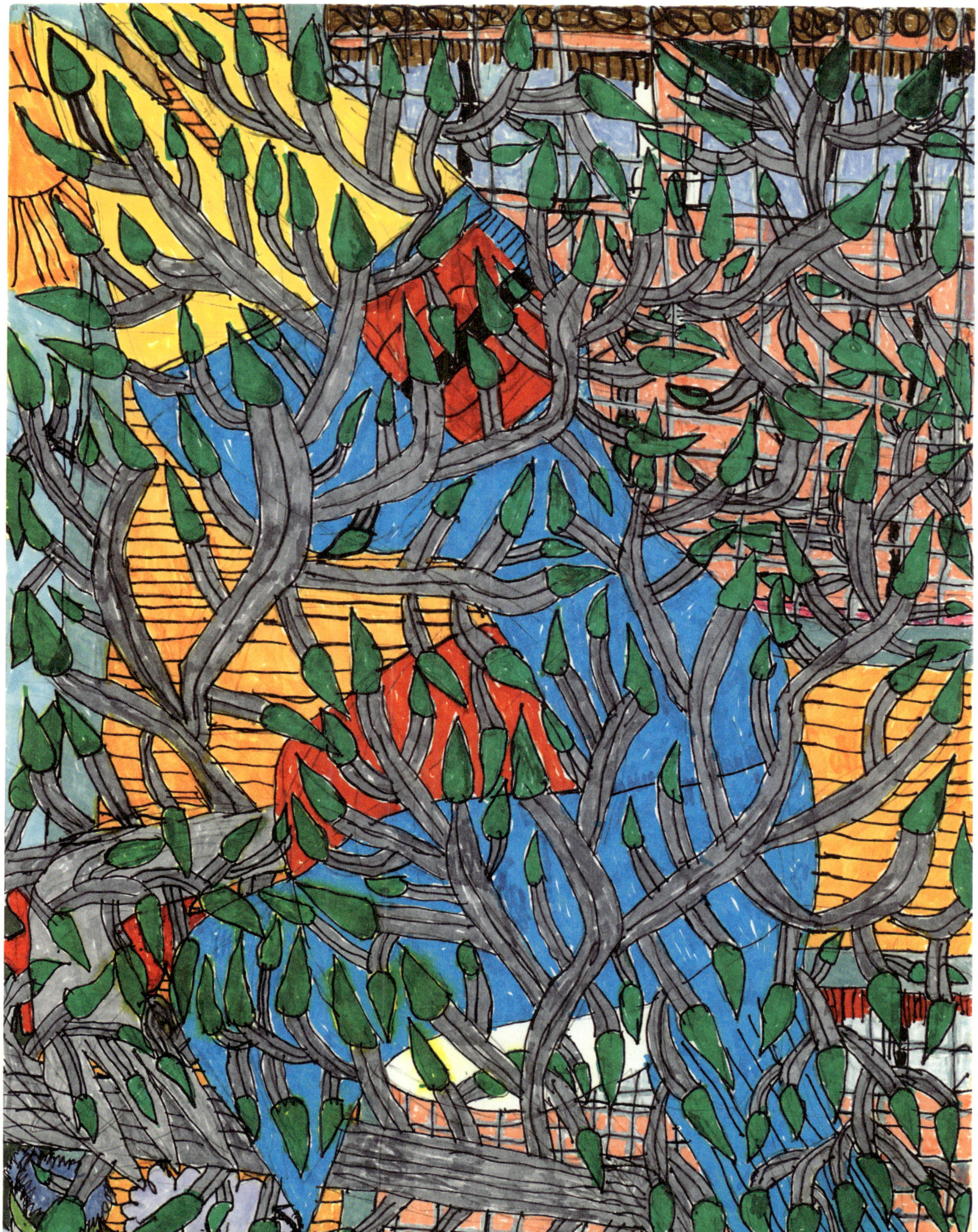

12 Untitled (Safari bus with cheetah)

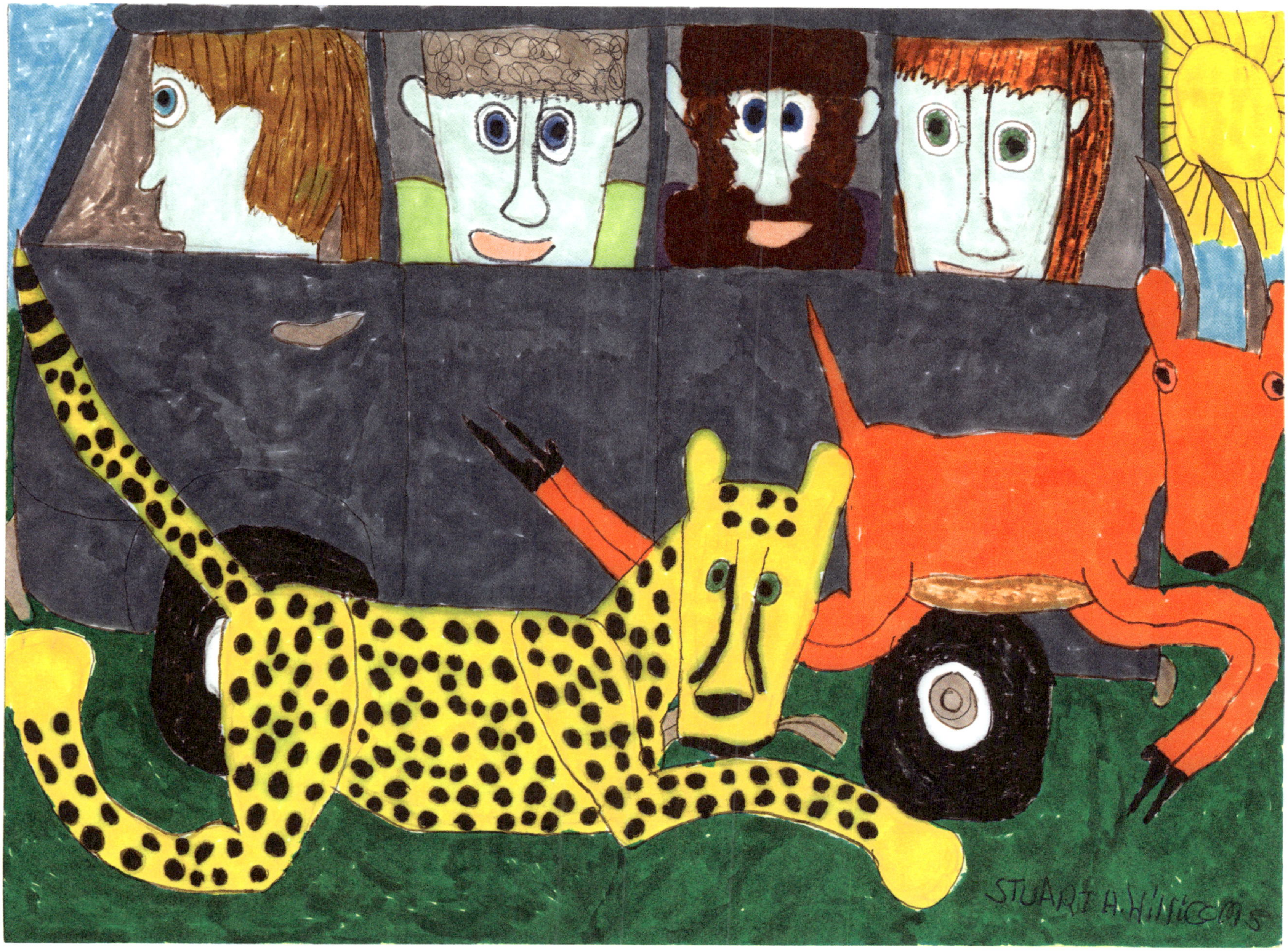
STUART H. WINICOMS

13 Untitled (Safari bus with lions)

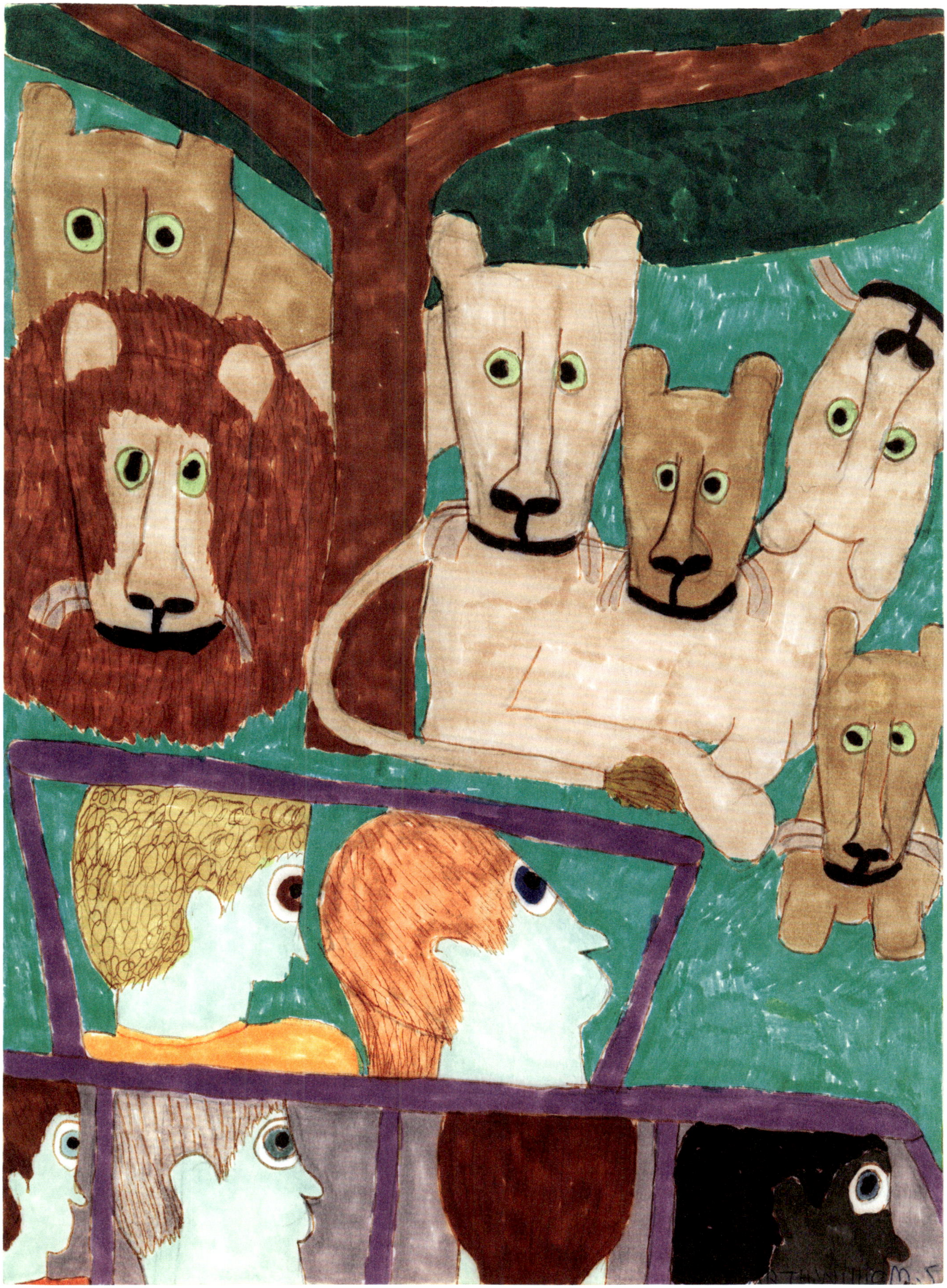

14 Untitled (We are three hungry foxes on the prowl)

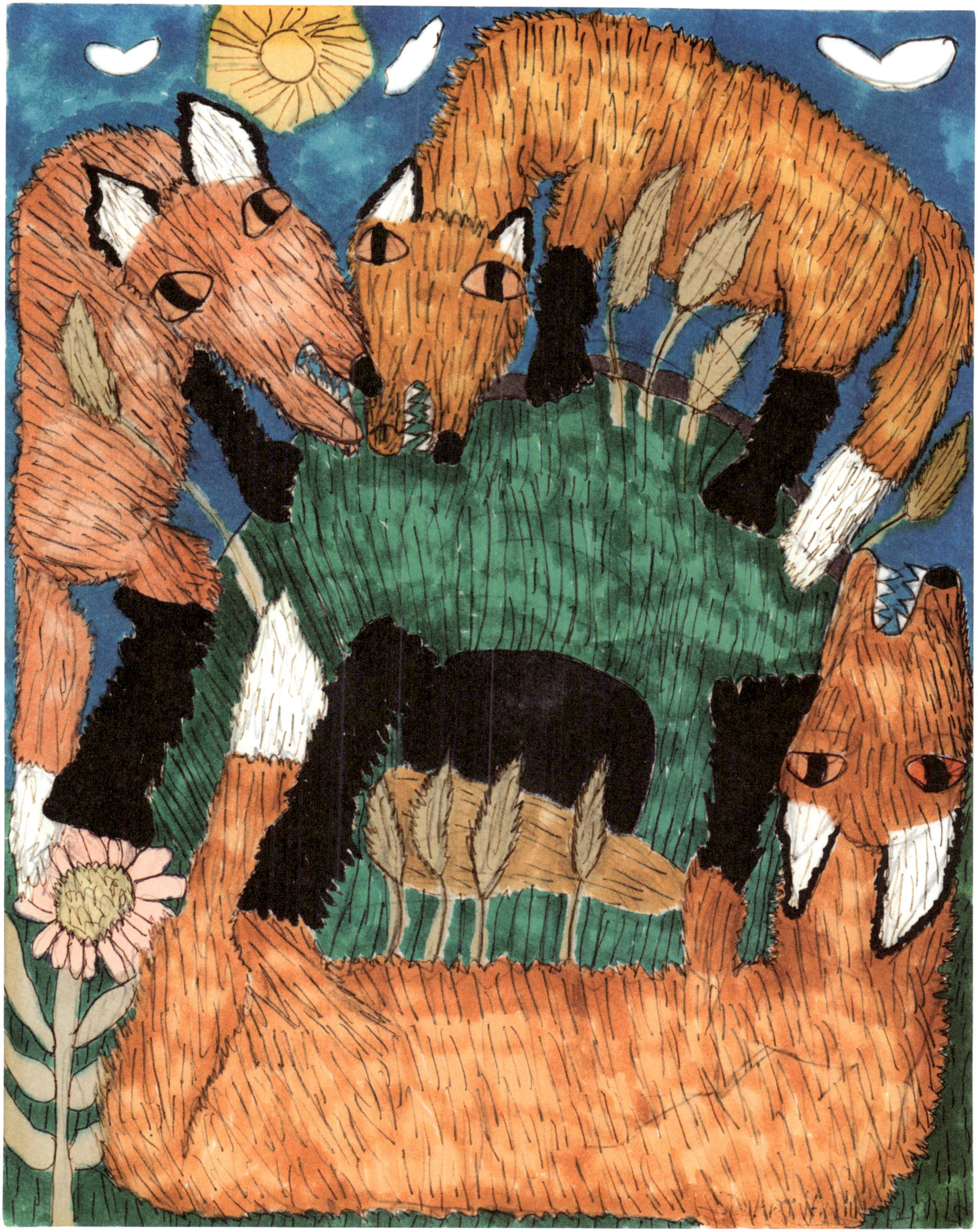

15 Untitled (Gorilla eating banana)

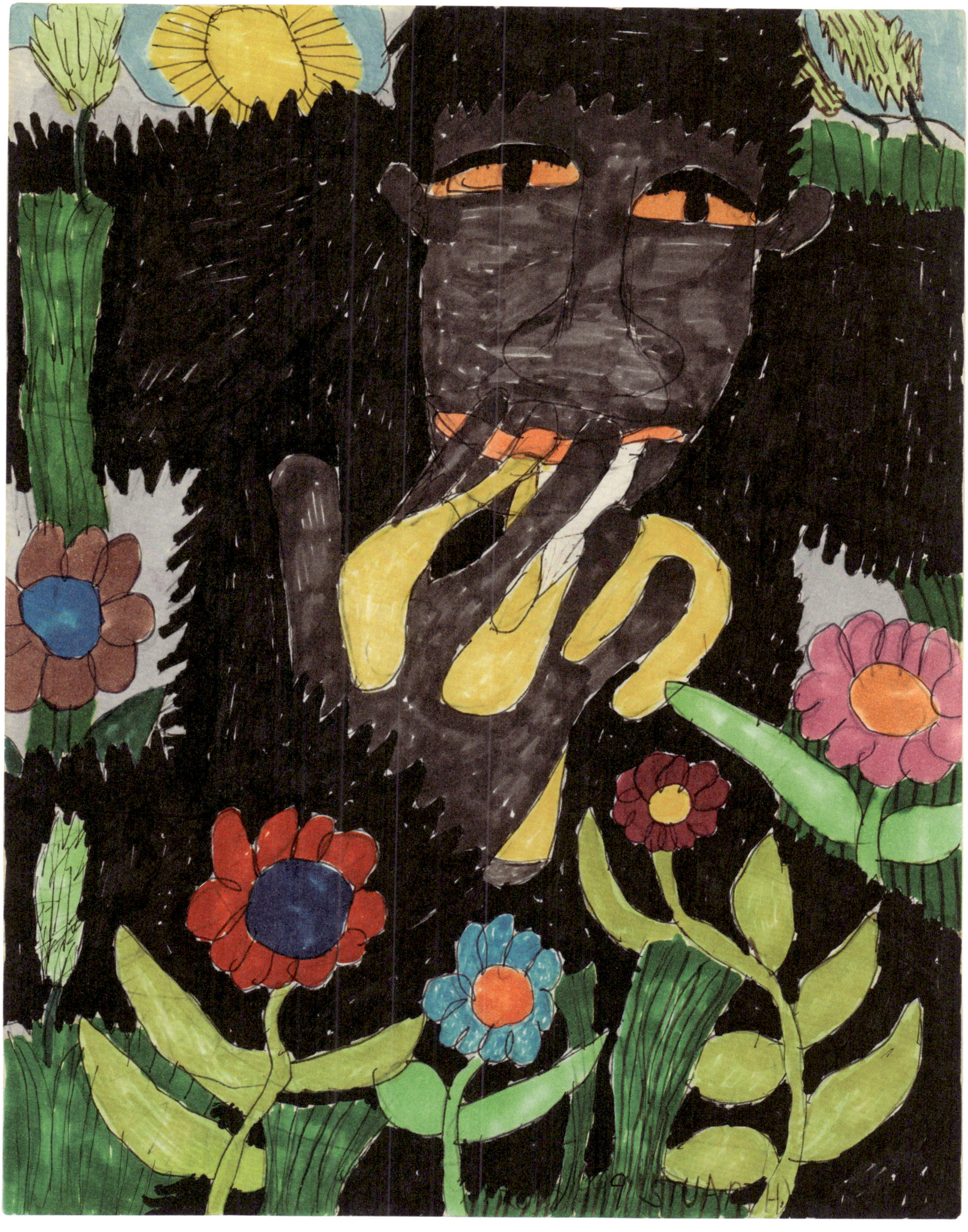
STUART H.

16 Lively Staircase

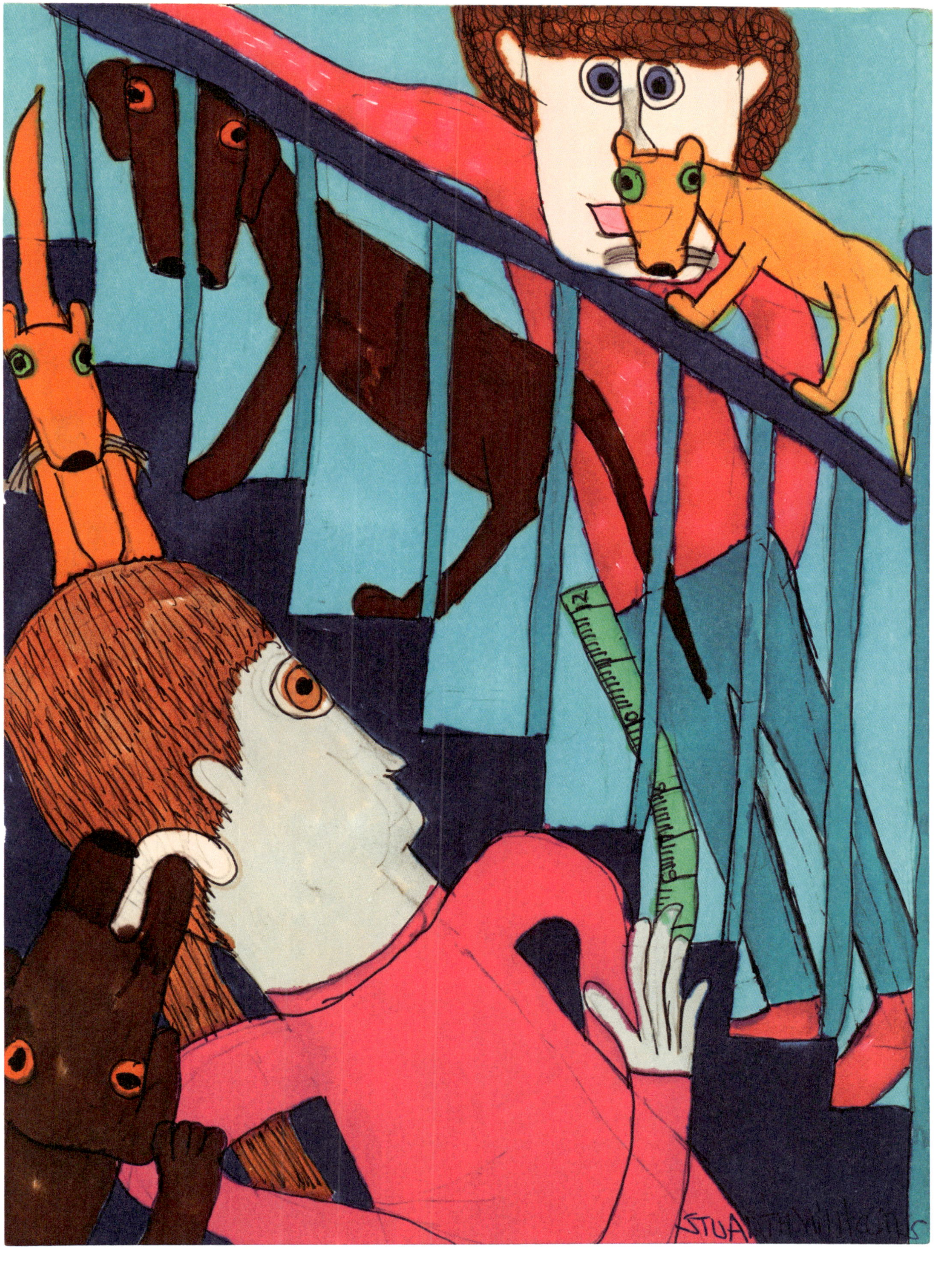

17 Untitled (Woodpecker)

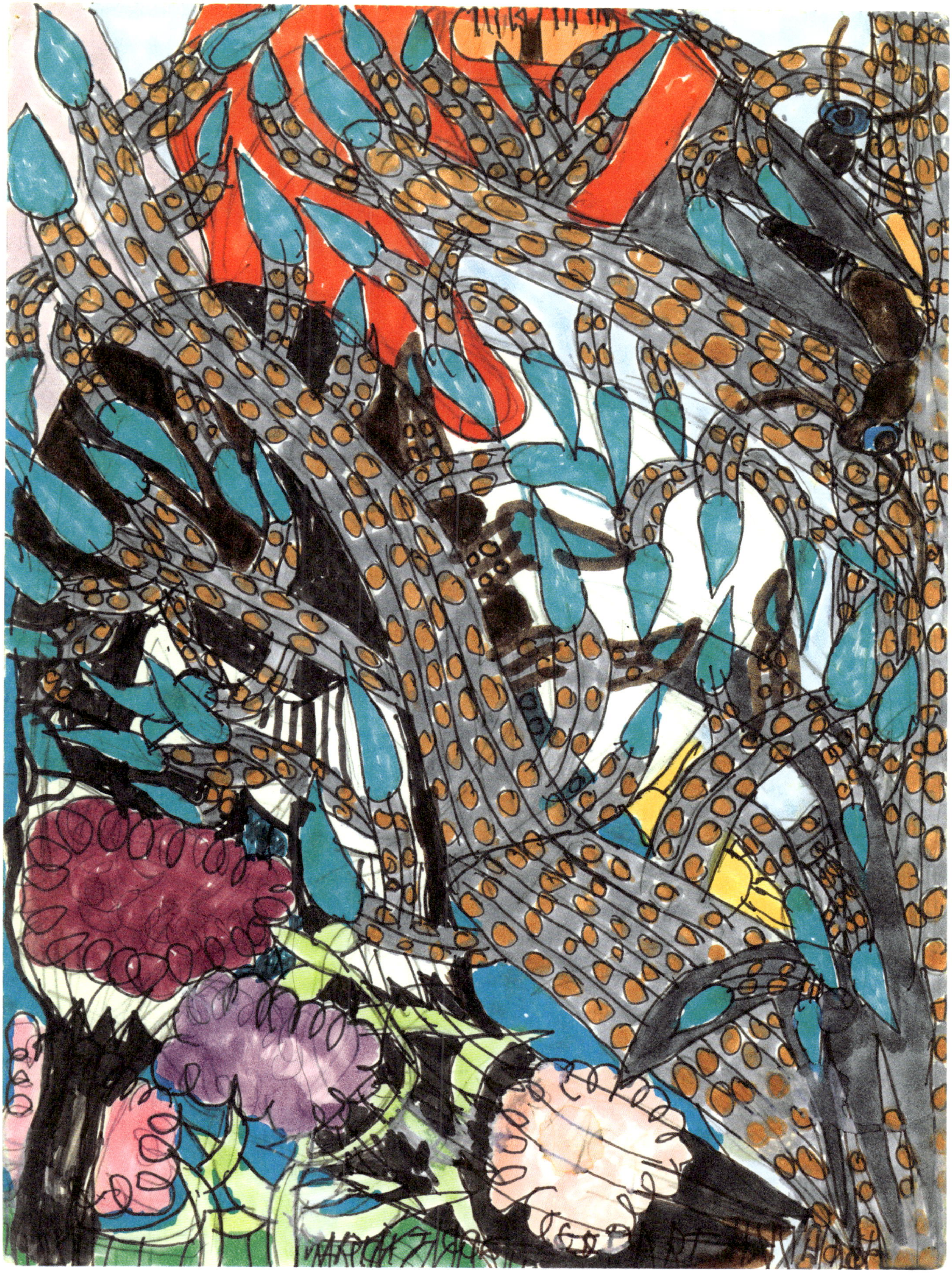

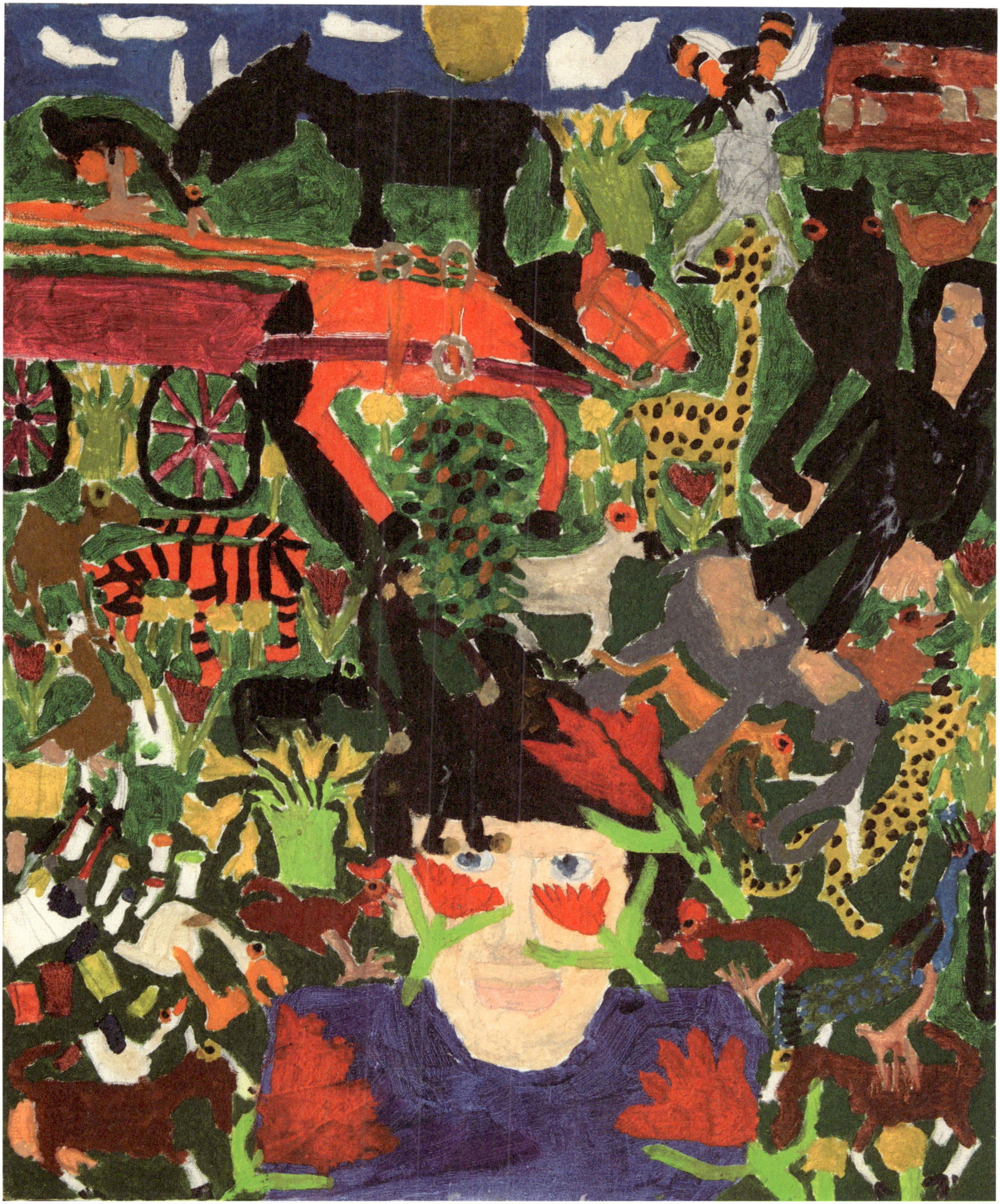

19 Untitled (Blue barn)

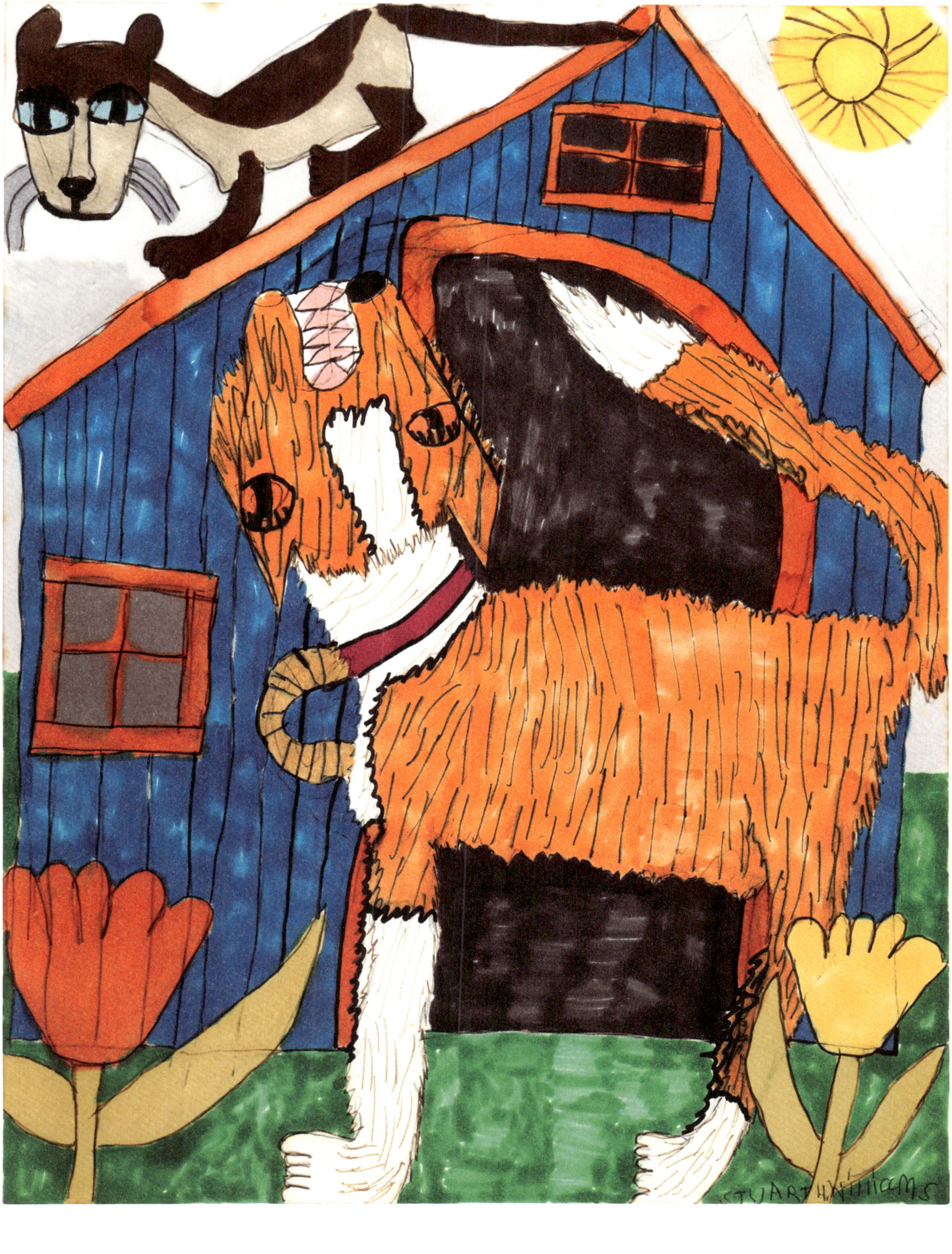
STUART H. Williams

20 Untitled (Figure with animals)

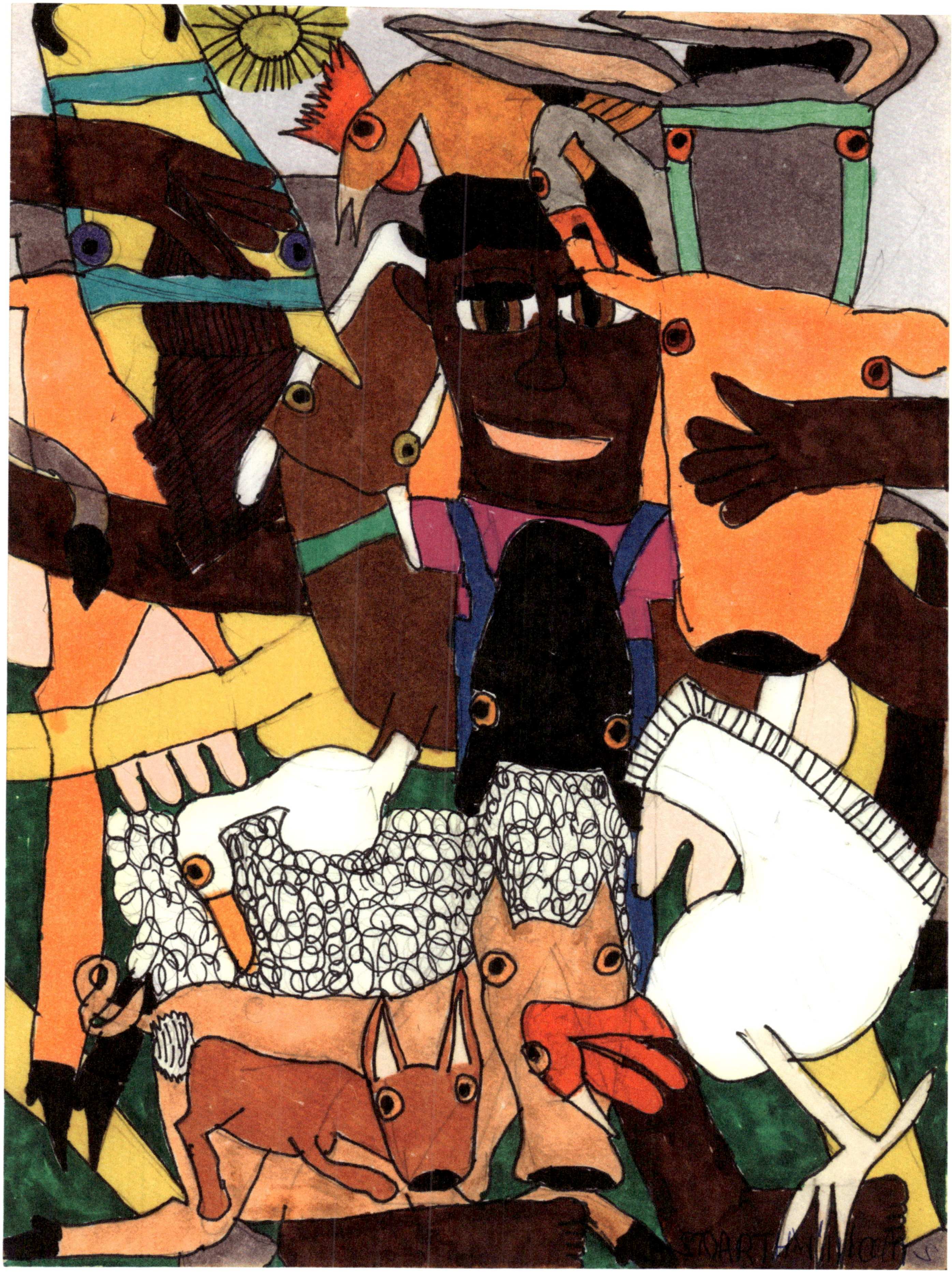

21 Untitled (Figures in purple sleigh)

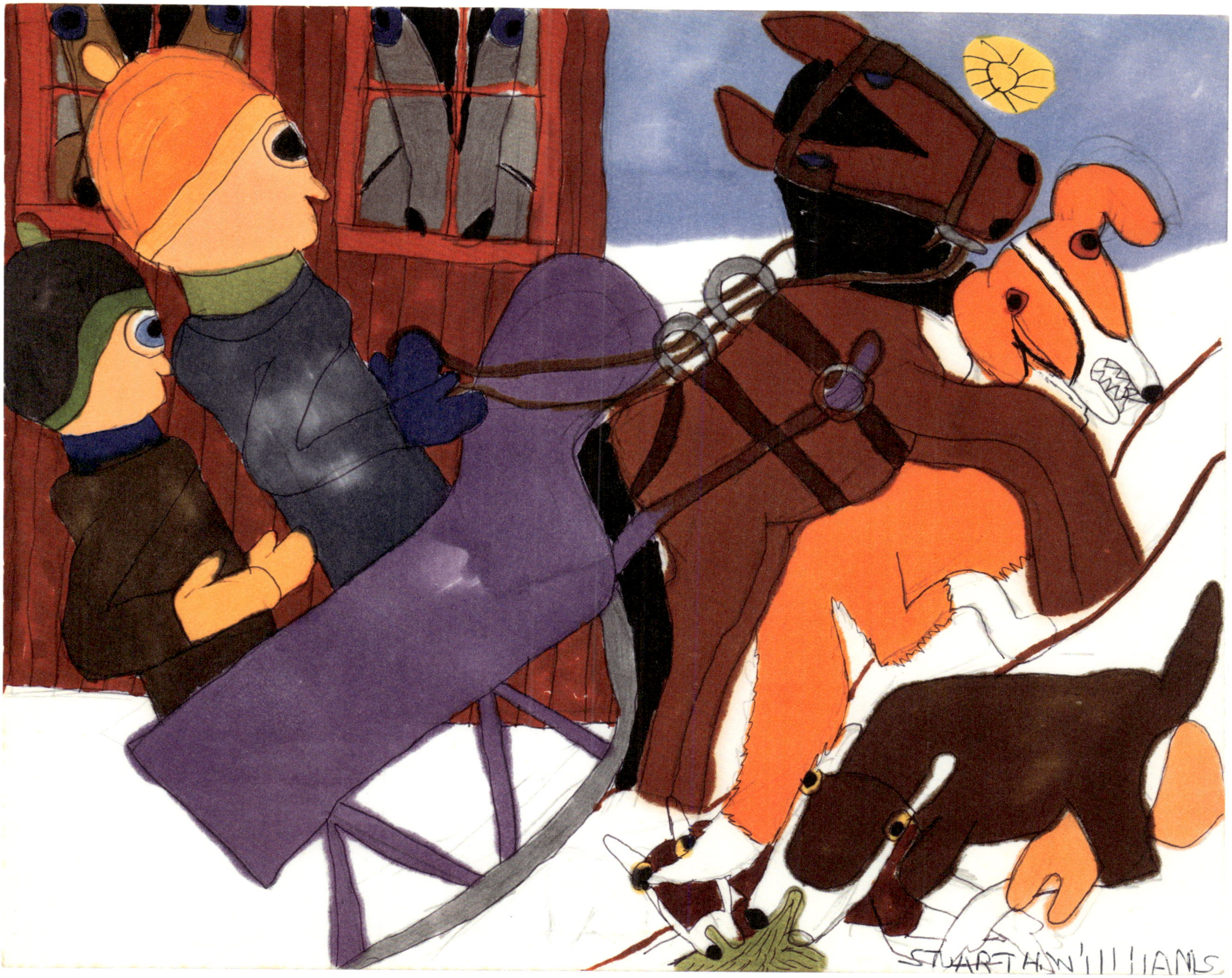
STUART H. WILLIAMS

22 Untitled (Big 40 birthday)

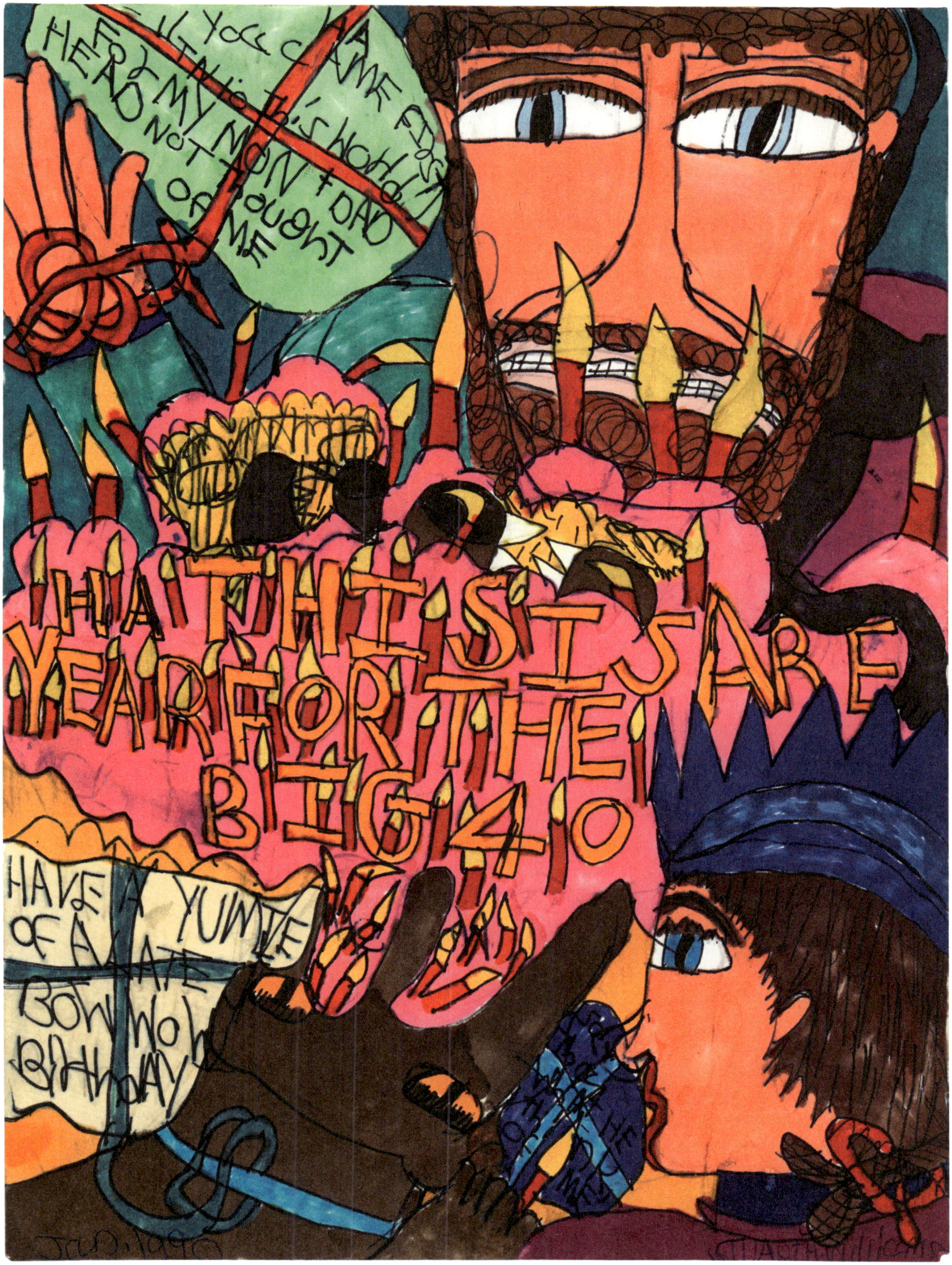

HA THIS IS ARE
YEAR FOR THE
BIG 40
HAVE A YUMIE
OF A ATE
BOW WOW
BIRTHDAY

23 Untitled (Figure with barn animals)

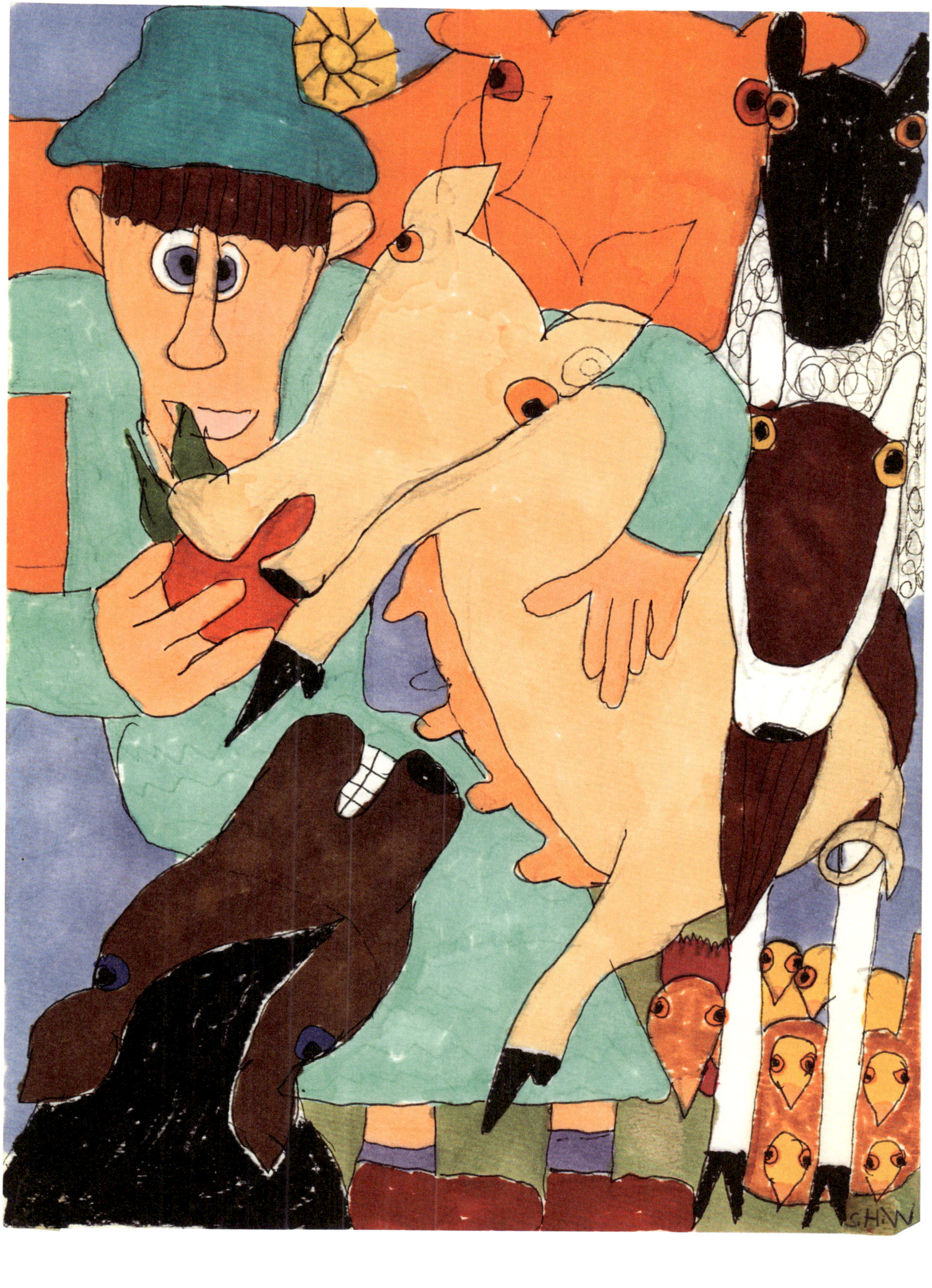
S.H.W

24 Untitled (Cat and dogs on steps)

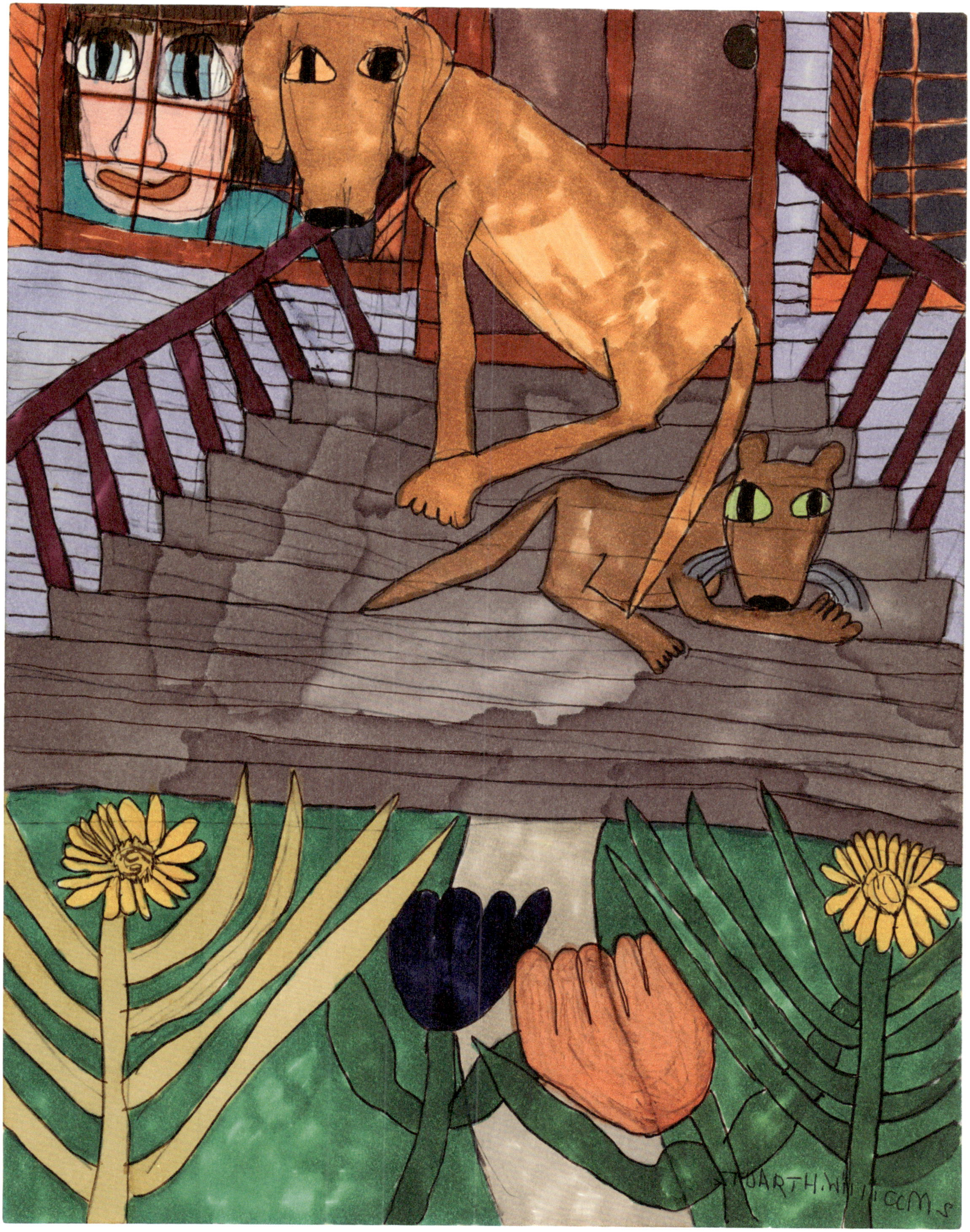

25 Untitled (Owl)

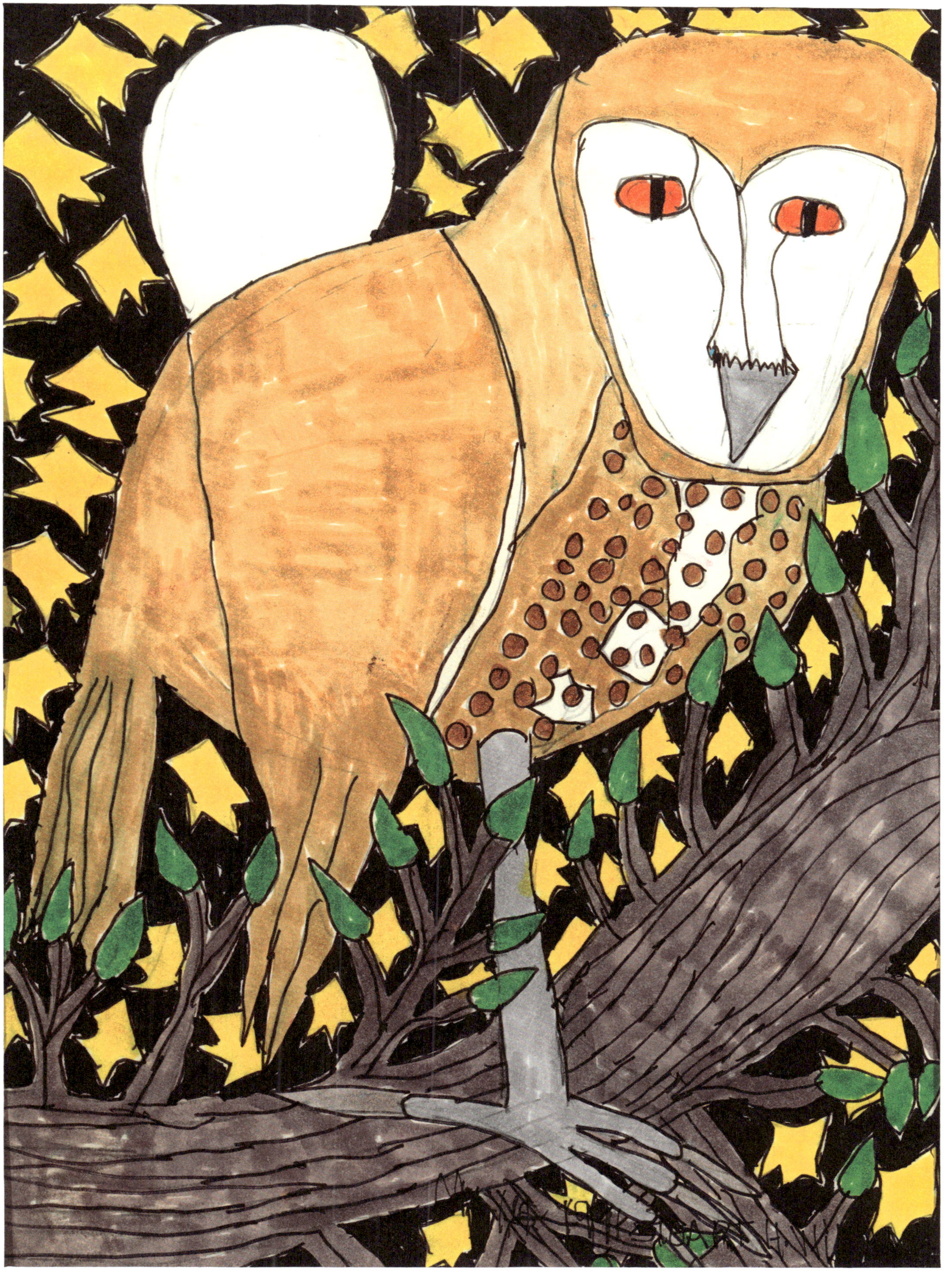

26 Galloping Through the Wild Flowers, Stumbled Upon a Honeybees Nest

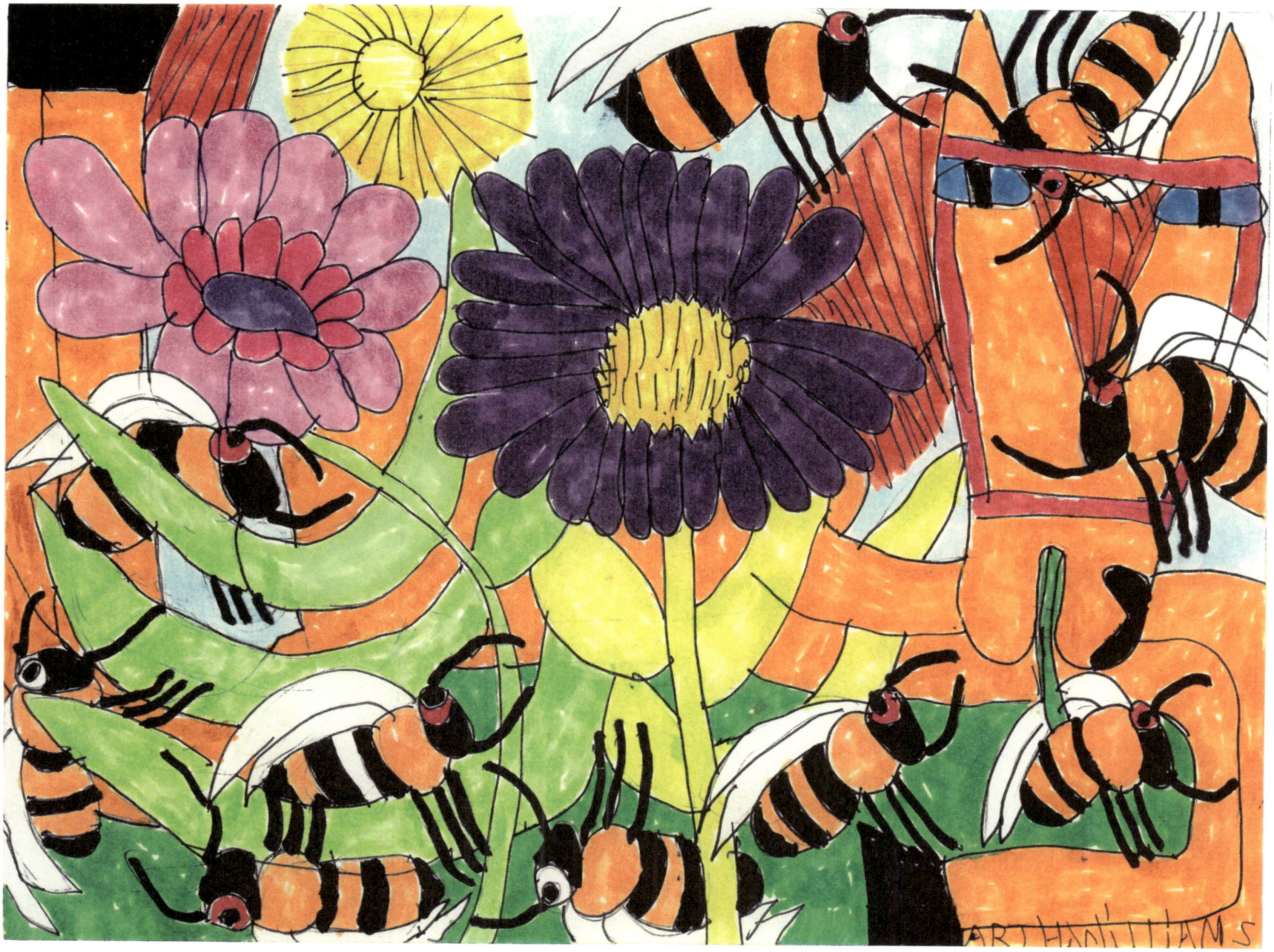

27 Untitled (Safari animals)

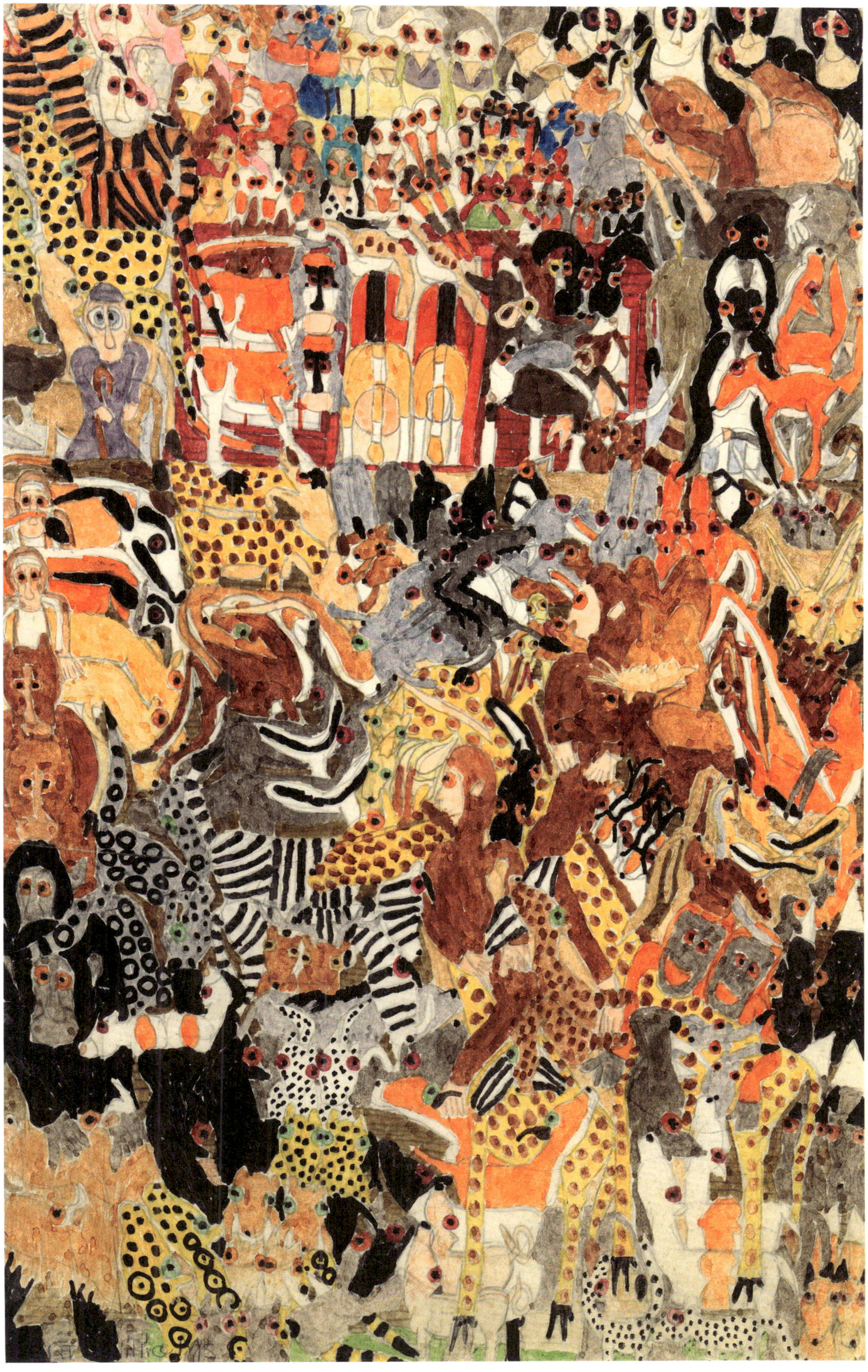

28 Untitled (Black bird)

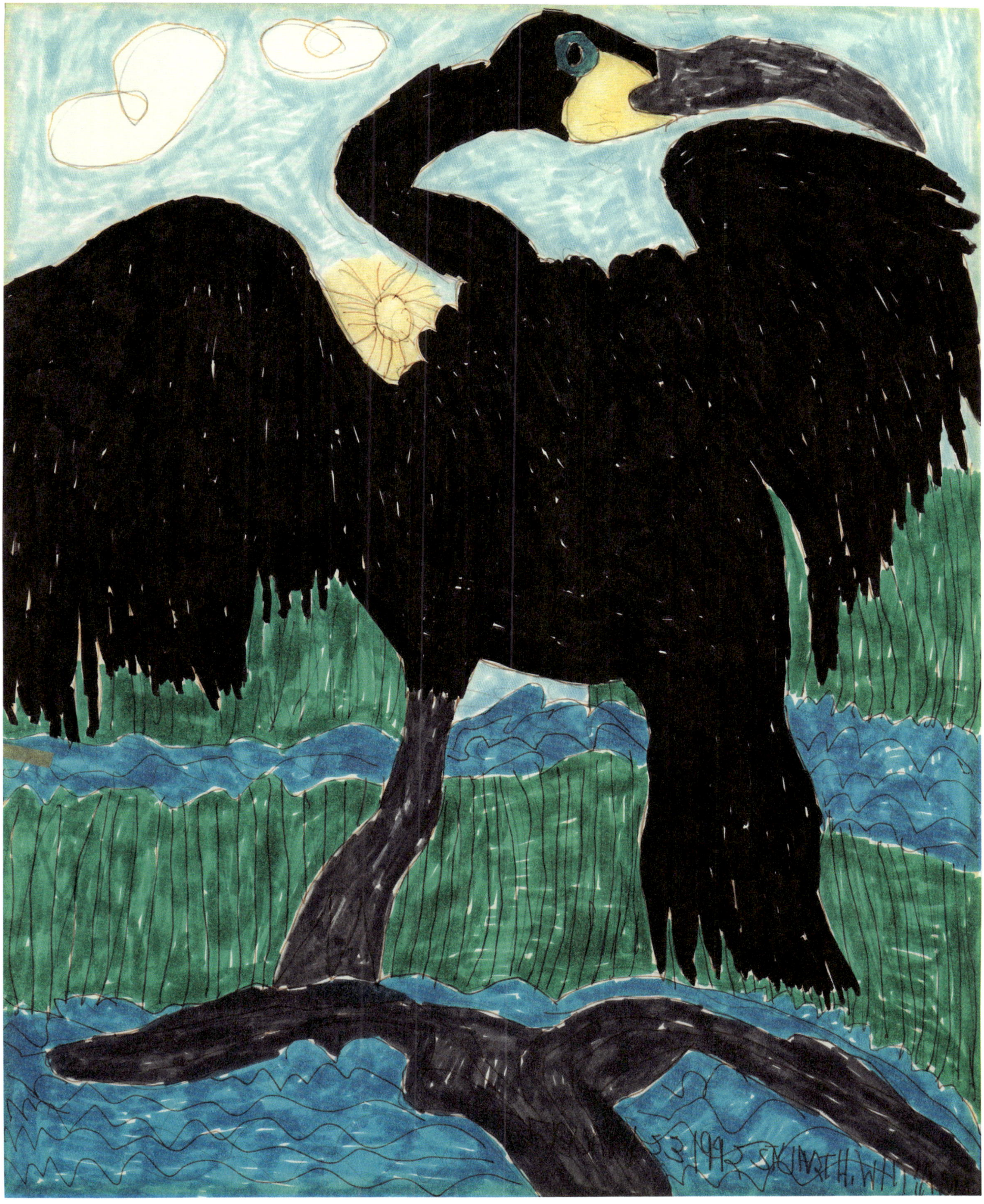
5 3 1992

29 Untitled (Animal-people at window)

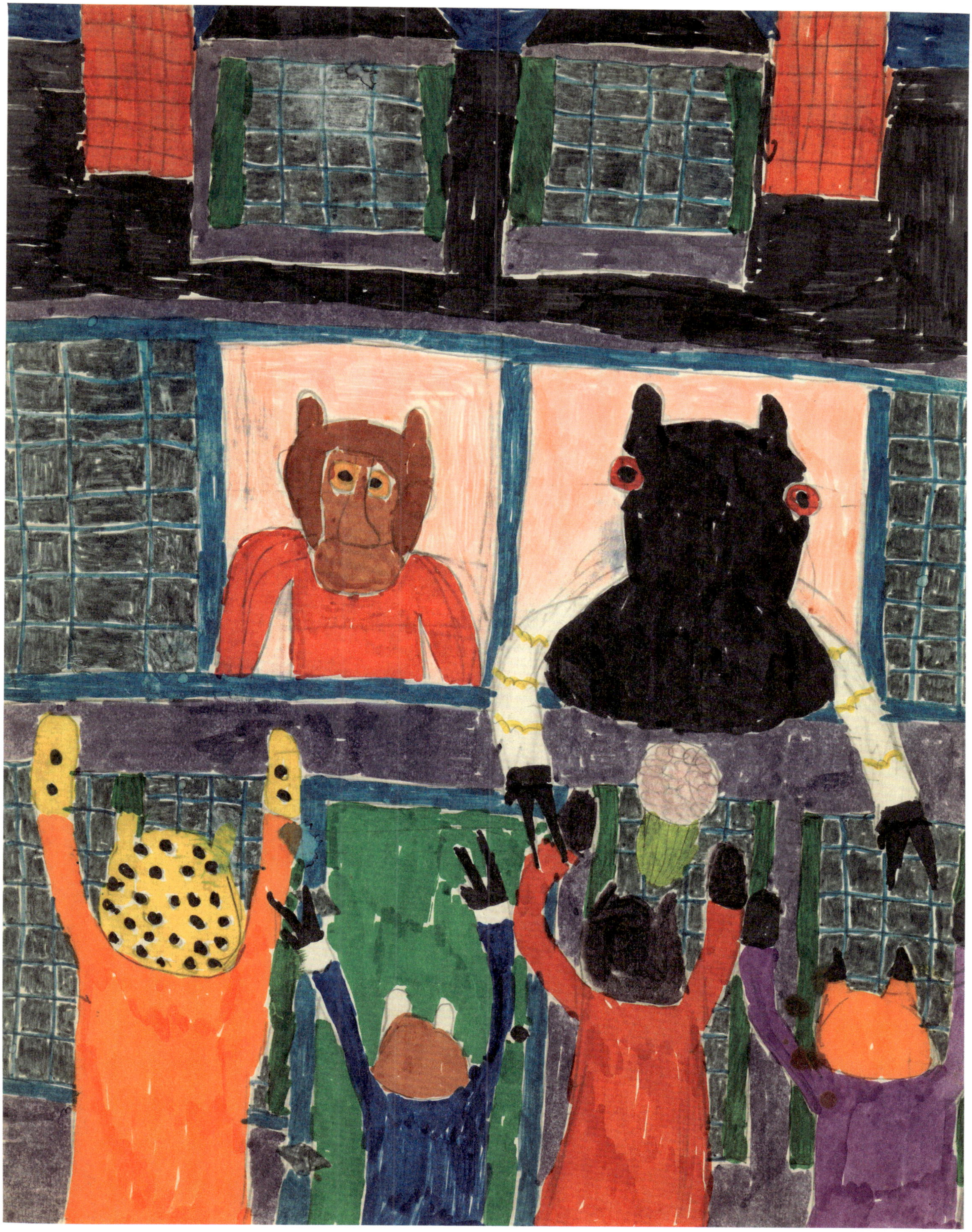

30 Animals Flying Over Barn

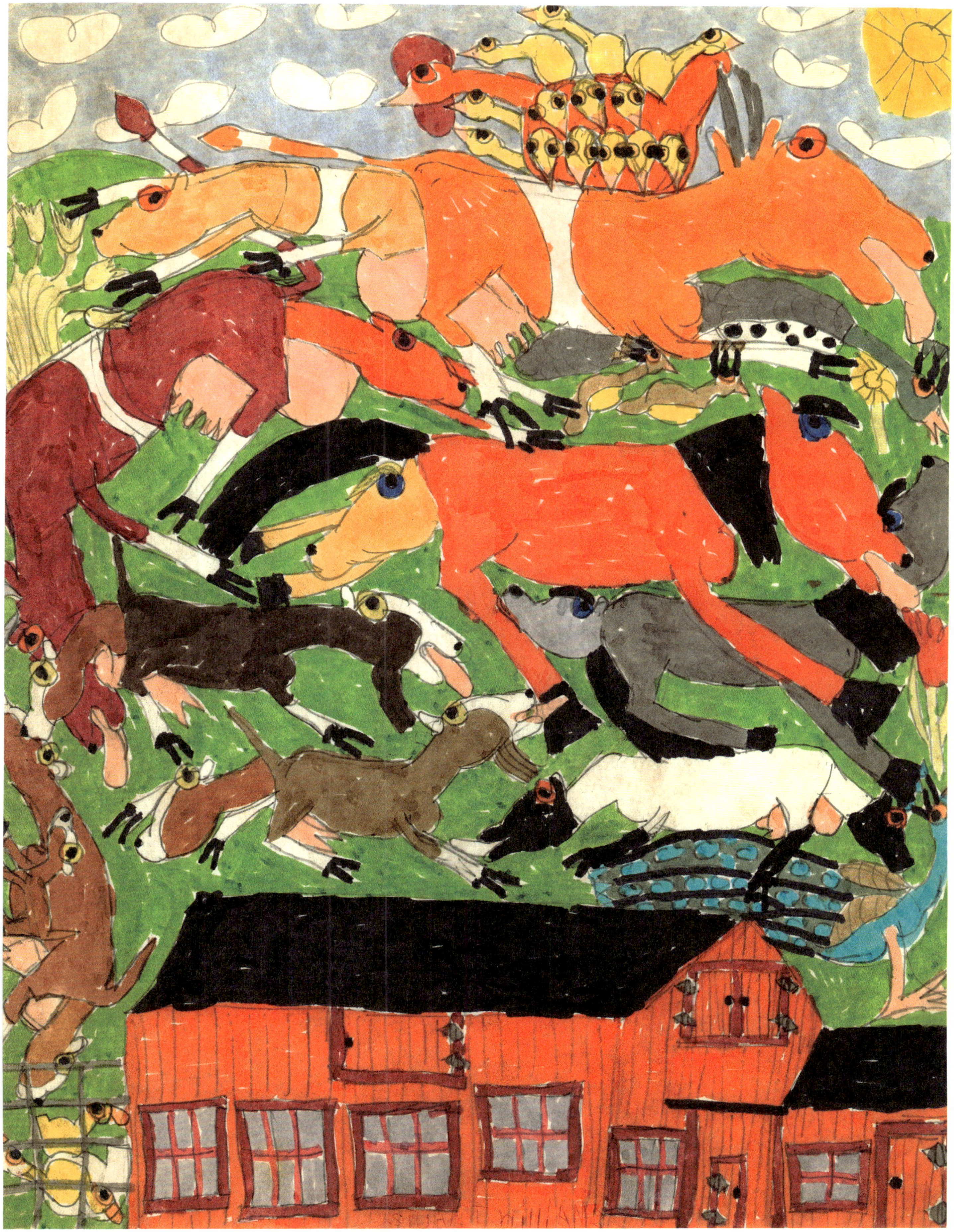

31 Untitled (Squirrel and nest of birds)

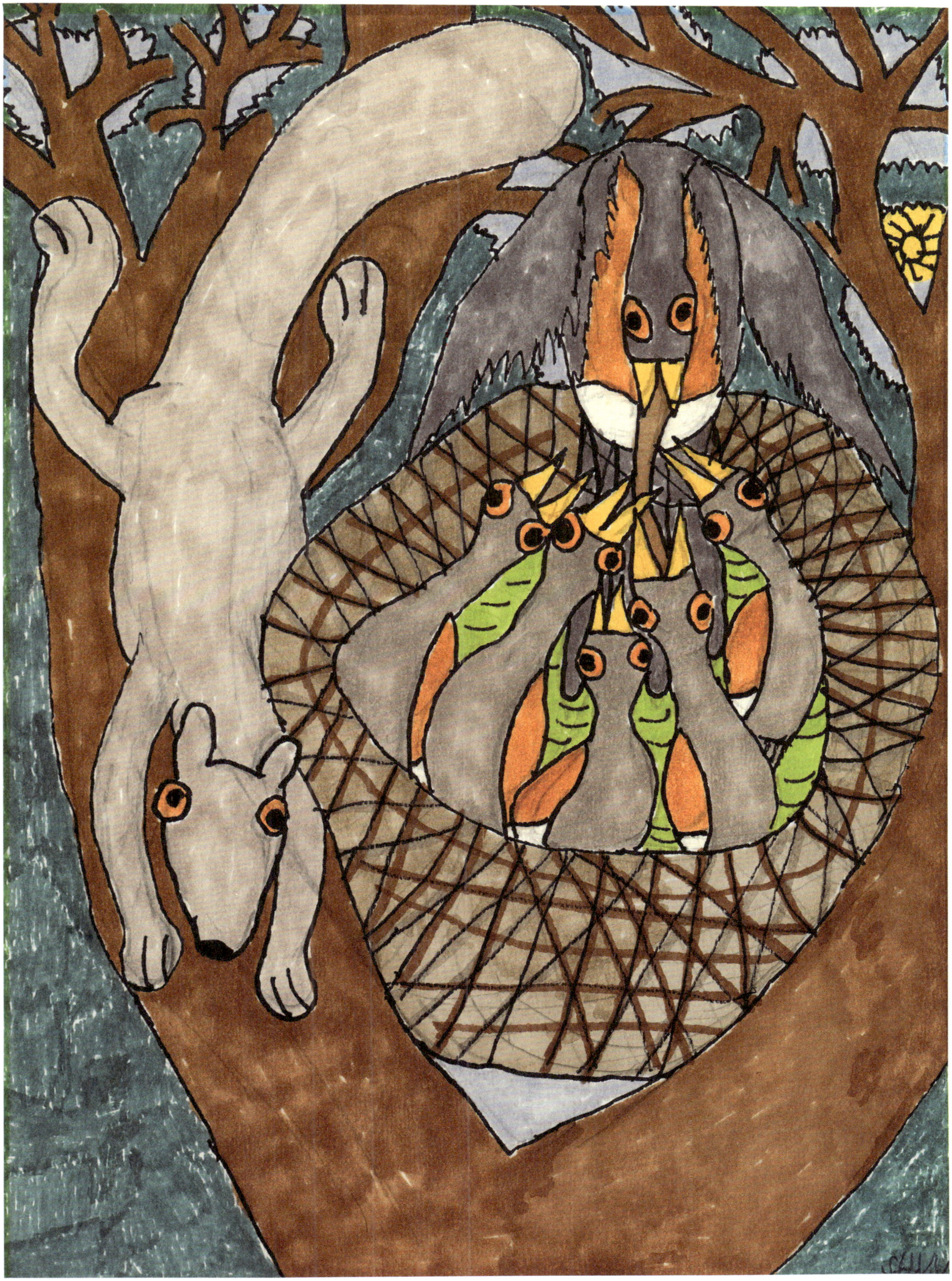

32 Untitled (Family, animals and tree on sled)

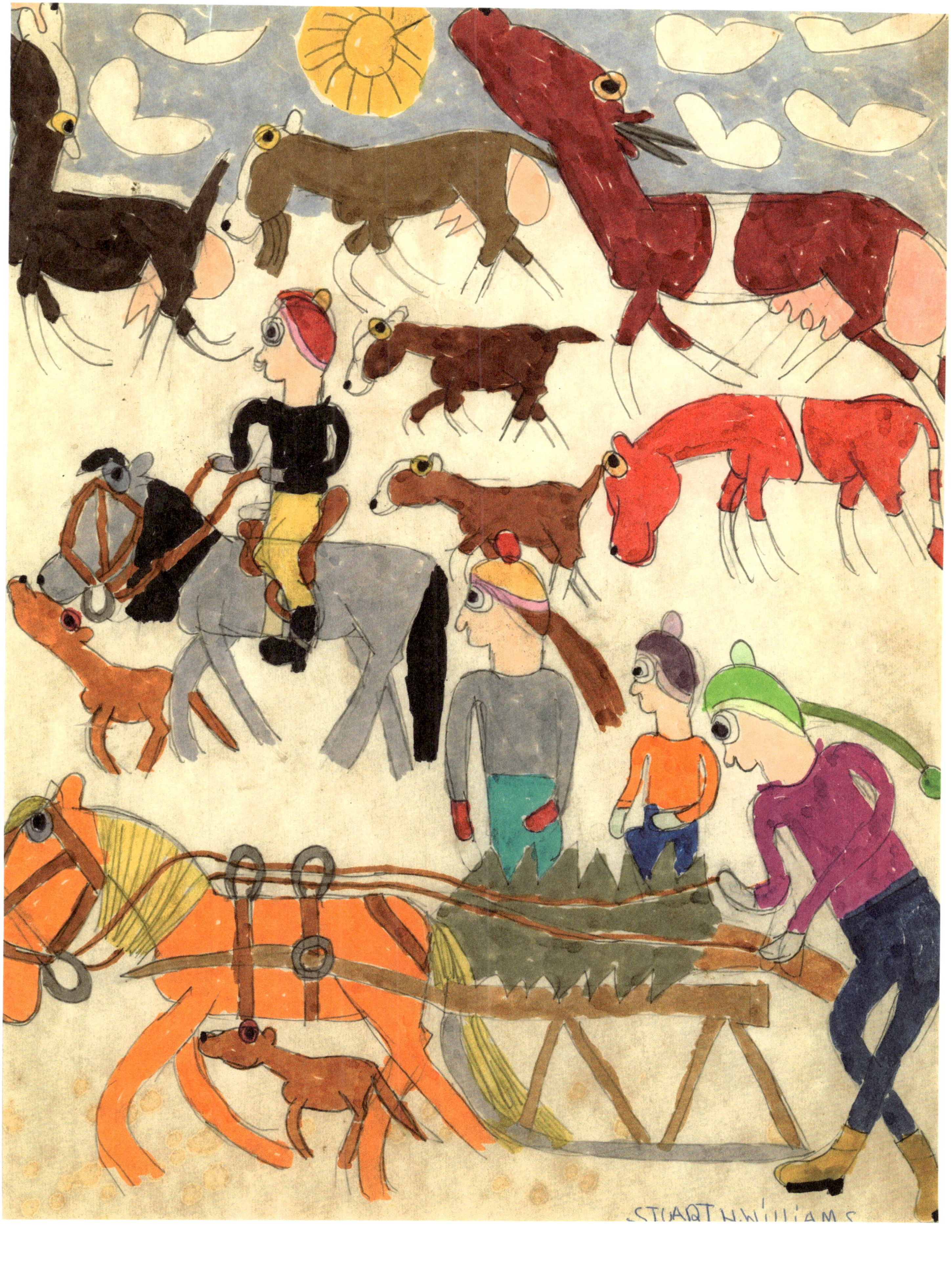
STUART H. WILLIAMS

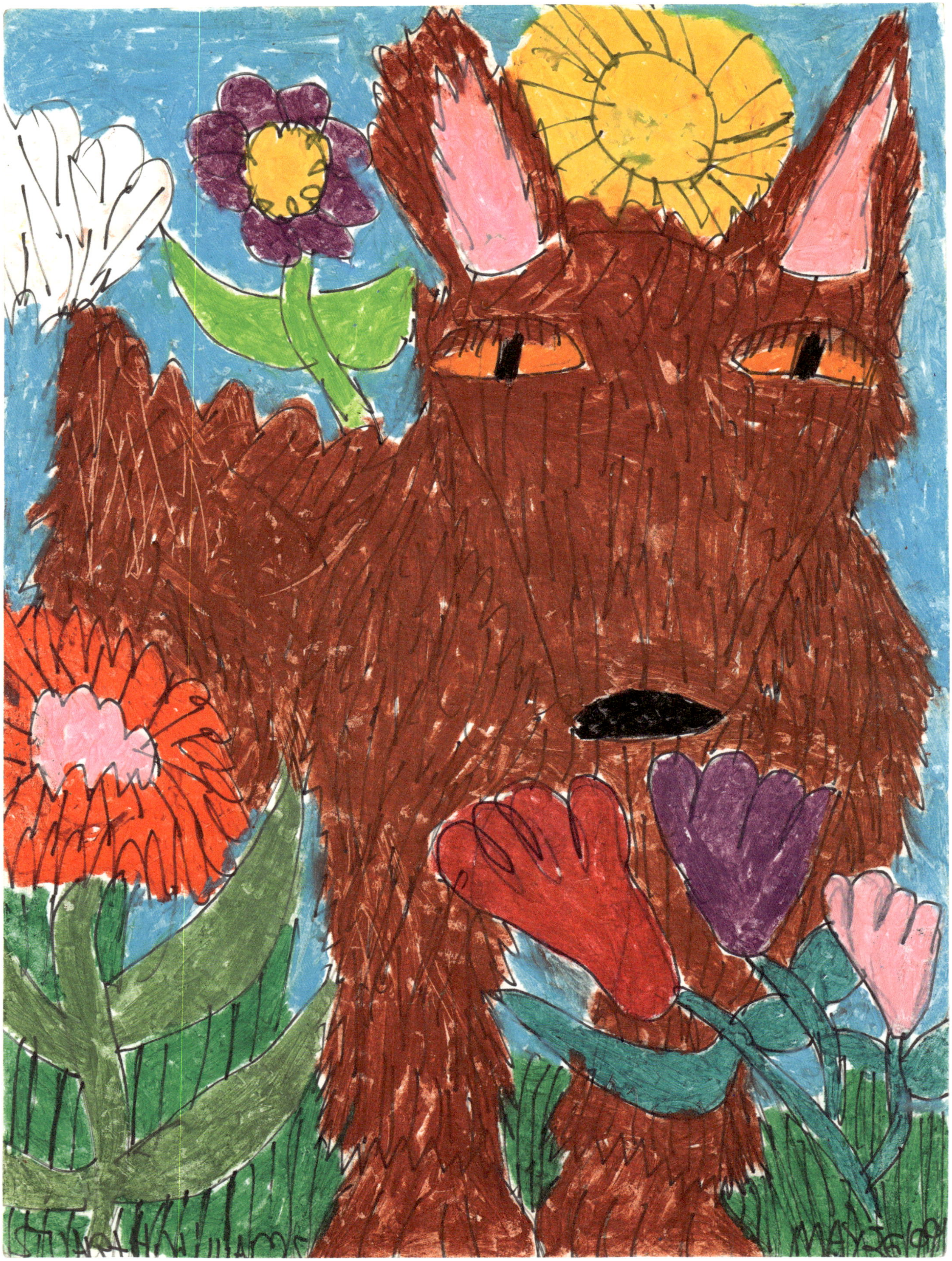

Chronology

1950 December 2: Stuart Hotchkiss Williams is born to Sydney Williams and Mary Hotchkiss Williams in Peterborough, New Hampshire, the seventh of nine children. Stuart is born with Prader–Willi Syndrome, but a disorder that has yet to be clinically identified.

1955/6 Stuart's father encourages him to care for the Toggenburg goats kept by the Williams family. Stuart will maintain a herd of these goats until 1996.

1956 Stuart enters Miss Linderman's Gosling School in Peterborough. He will attend the school through 1970. Because of its distance from the Dodge Place (the Williams family home) and Stuart's difficulty with walking, he will be driven to the school throughout his years there.

Prader–Willi is first described by Andrea Prader and Heinrich Willi; however, the syndrome's identification will not become general knowledge for many years.

1963 Stuart's mother takes him to the Sharon Art Center in Sharon, New Hampshire, where he has lessons sporadically over two years with the artists Bea Orchard and Fleur Weymouth.

1966 The first Monadnock Music Festival is held in Peterborough. Over the years, Stuart will frequently show his art at their annual Christmas fairs.

1968 December 2: On Stuart's eighteenth birthday, his father, Sydney Williams, dies of lung cancer at age fifty-eight.

1970 Stuart's fourteenth and last year at the Gosling School.

1971 His sister Jenny takes Stuart to Switzerland to see Toggenburg goats in their native habitat.

1972 Stuart's sister Jenny and younger brother Willard open the Toadstool Bookshop in Peterborough. The shop will display Stuart's art and sell his Christmas cards, postcards, and calendars.

Stuart completes an eight-by-six-foot mural for Jim Haddock's Monadnock Family Services office in Keene, New Hampshire. The theme is a working farm. In 1992 the mural is transferred to the Monadnock Children's Museum in Keene. The museum has since closed; the whereabouts of the mural are unknown.

1975 The Iselin family opens the Folkways Café on Grove Street in the center of Peterborough. Over the twenty-one years of its existence, the Folkways frequently displays Stuart's art.

1977 Jenny takes Stuart on a two-week trip to Africa. They spend the first week in Egypt and the second week touring game parks in Tanzania and Kenya.

1970s At some point in the decade, Stuart's older sister Mary reads an article in the *Boston Globe* describing Prader–Willi; she recognizes this as Stuart's condition.

"This is the drawing I bought from Stuart when I visited him at the Hill Resource Center in Abilene. I think of Stuart as something of a sly fox." —*William Corbett*

1970s (*cont.*) Also during this period, Stuart is taken to Boston to be fitted for special boots and metal braces. He will wear such boots for the rest of his life.

1986 January: Stuart's niece Robina Gregg (now O'Rourke), age nineteen, takes him on a three-week trip to Kenya and Tanzania. They travel through various wildlife parks and across the Serengeti plains.

November 25–December 26: *The World of Stuart Williams,* curated by Robert "Mac" Doty, at the Currier Museum of Art in Manchester, New Hampshire.

1989 Mac Doty selects a picture by Stuart for the Currier Museum of Art exhibition *By Good Hands: New Hampshire Folk Art.* Exhibition runs through the summer.

1990 December 1: *The Williams Family, Yesterday and Today*, showing the art of Stuart's parents, Sydney and Mary, and Stuart, opens.

December 2: On Stuart's thirty-eighth birthday, Mary Williams dies in her sleep.

After their mother's death the Williams siblings hold a family meeting to assess how to best care for and support Stuart. His sister Betsy volunteers to take him into her New Boston, New Hampshire, home. This arrangement lasts for three months. Stuart then returns briefly to the Dodge Place, where a breakdown sends him to McLean Hospital in Lexington, Massachusetts, and then into the psychiatric unit at New York Hospital in White Plains, New York. Stuart leaves there for a series of group homes in and around Peterborough; most significantly, at the home of Stuart and Juliann Weeks in Temple, New Hampshire. He also lives independently in a house on Thorndike Pond in Jaffrey, New Hampshire. During this seventeen-year period before he moves to Abilene, Texas, his movements have proved impossible to track precisely.

1991 June: Shaw Gallery in Keene, New Hampshire, shows Stuart's work so successfully that the gallery gives him a second show, in 1992.

1992 Stuart moves into the home of Stuart and Juliann Weeks, where he meets and befriends John Eisenman, who will assist him in moving to Abilene, Texas.

1994 *Perspectives*, the magazine of the Prader–Willi Syndrome Association, hosts Stuart as Man of the Year at its convention in Scottsdale, Arizona.

1995 July–September: Stuart exhibits at Yale University's Connecticut Mental Health Center in New Haven, Connecticut.

1996 Stuart's last year as a goat keeper.

2000 Stuart exhibits at the Monadnock Music Christmas Fair for the last time.

2001 Summer: *Man's Best Friend*, a one-man show at the Civic Center in Jaffrey, New Hampshire.

October 6: Stuart opens the Creature Art gallery to sell his work. It closes after six weeks.

2003 December 6–January 17, 2004: One-man show at Boston's Nielsen Gallery.

2006 February 21–March 18: One-man show at Manhattan's Davis & Langdale Company.

2007 Stuart moves to Abilene, Texas, where he eventually takes up residence at the Hill Resource Center.

2012 May 15: After a short illness, Stuart dies in Abilene. He is buried beside his parents and paternal grandparents in the family plot at Peterborough's Pine Hill Cemetery.

2014 March 9–May 18: *Stuart H. Williams, Looking Through All Over*, an exhibition held as part of the Art and Healing series at the Danforth Art museum in Framingham, Massachusetts. Exhibition curator Adrienne Jacobson writes the wall texts for Stuart's drawings and gives a gallery talk. (Stuart often signed his work Stuart H. Williams, but he published his calendars and usually exhibited under the name Stuart Williams.)

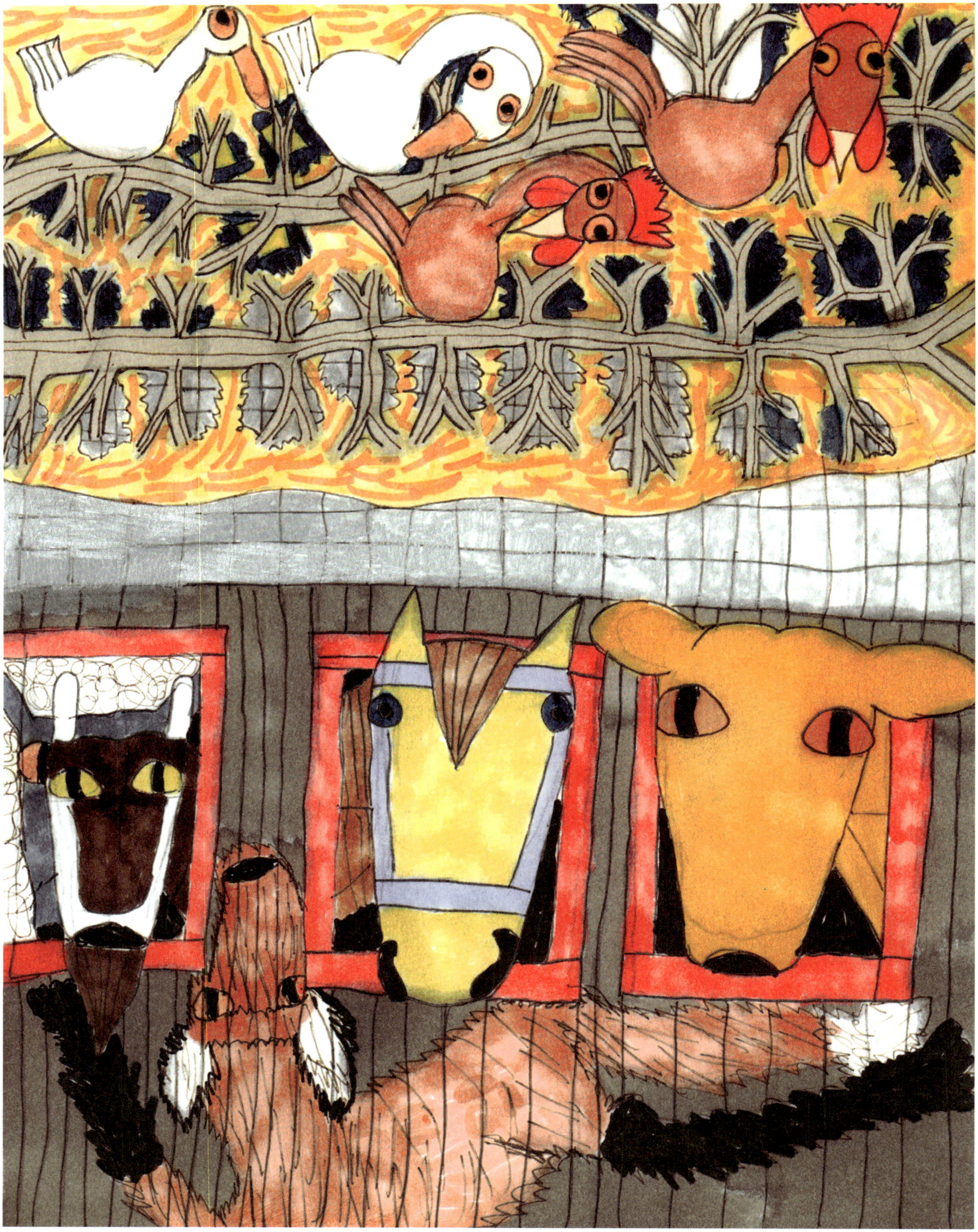

List of Plates

The nosy fox looks up at the goat, horse, and cow looking out, a theme of Stuart's, to view the world. Aloft, ducks and chickens in tree limbs are delectable, like grapes to a hungry fox.

11 *Untitled (It is a beautiful spring day here in Milford, N.H.)*
1994
Marker, ink, and pencil on paper
14 × 10½ inches
Collection of Frank Williams

12 *Untitled (Safari bus with cheetah)*
No date
Marker and ink on paper
15 × 11 inches
Collection of Frank Williams

13 *Untitled (Safari bus with lions)*
No date
Marker and ink on paper
15 × 11 inches
Collection of Frank Williams

14 *Untitled (We are three hungry foxes on the prowl)*
No date
Marker and ink on paper
14 × 11 inches
Collection of Frank Williams

15 *Untitled (Gorilla eating banana)*
No date
Marker and ink on paper
14 × 11 inches
Collection of Frank Williams

16 *Lively Staircase*
No date
Marker, ink, and pencil on paper
12 × 9 inches
Collection of Louisa Shibli

17 *Untitled (Woodpecker)*
1995
Marker, ink, and pencil on paper
12 × 9 inches
Collection of Fleur Weymouth

18 *The Farmer's Dream*
Early 1970s
Oil paint on canvas
4 × 20 inches
Collection of Noah Sobe

19 *Untitled (Blue barn)*
No date
Marker, ink, and pencil on paper
14 × 11 inches
Collection of Sue Martin

20 *Untitled (Figure with animals)*
No date
Marker, ink, and pencil on paper)
12 × 9 inches
Collection of Sue Martin

21 *Untitled (Figures in purple sleigh)*
No date
Marker, ink, and pencil on paper
11 × 14 inches
Collection of Sue Martin

22 *Untitled (Big 40 birthday)*
1990
Marker, ink, and pencil on paper
12 × 9 inches
Collection of Sue Martin

23 *Untitled (Figure with barn animals)*
No date
Marker, ink, pencil, and watercolor on watercolor paper
12 × 9 inches
Collection of Sue Martin

24 *Untitled (Cat and dog on steps)*
No date
Marker, ink, and pencil on paper
14 × 11 inches
Collection of Sue Martin

25 *Untitled (Owl)*
No date
Marker on paper
11½ × 8½ inches
Collection of Caroline and William Featherstone

26 *Galloping Through the Wild Flowers, Stumbled Upon a Honeybees Nest*
No date
Marker, ink, and pencil on paper
11 × 14 inches
Collection of Sydney Williams

27 *Untitled (Safari animals)*
No date
Marker, ink, and pencil on paper
12 × 9 inches
Collection of Sydney Williams

28 *Untitled (Black bird)*
No date
Marker, ink, and pencil on paper
12 × 9 inches
Collection of Sydney Williams

29 *Untitled (Animal-people at window)*
No date
Marker and pencil on paper
13¼ × 10½ inches
Collection of Caroline and William Featherstone

30 *Animals flying over barn*
No date
Marker and pencil on paper
10¼ × 7½ inches
Collection of Melissa and Edward Williams

31 *Untitled (Squirrel and nest of birds)*
No date
Marker and pencil on paper
12 × 9 inches
Collection of Melissa and Edward Williams

32 *Untitled (Family, animals and tree on sled)*
No date
Marker, ink, and pencil on paper
10½ × 7½ inches
Collection of Sydney Williams

Printed by GHP Media
Design and typography by Michael Russem

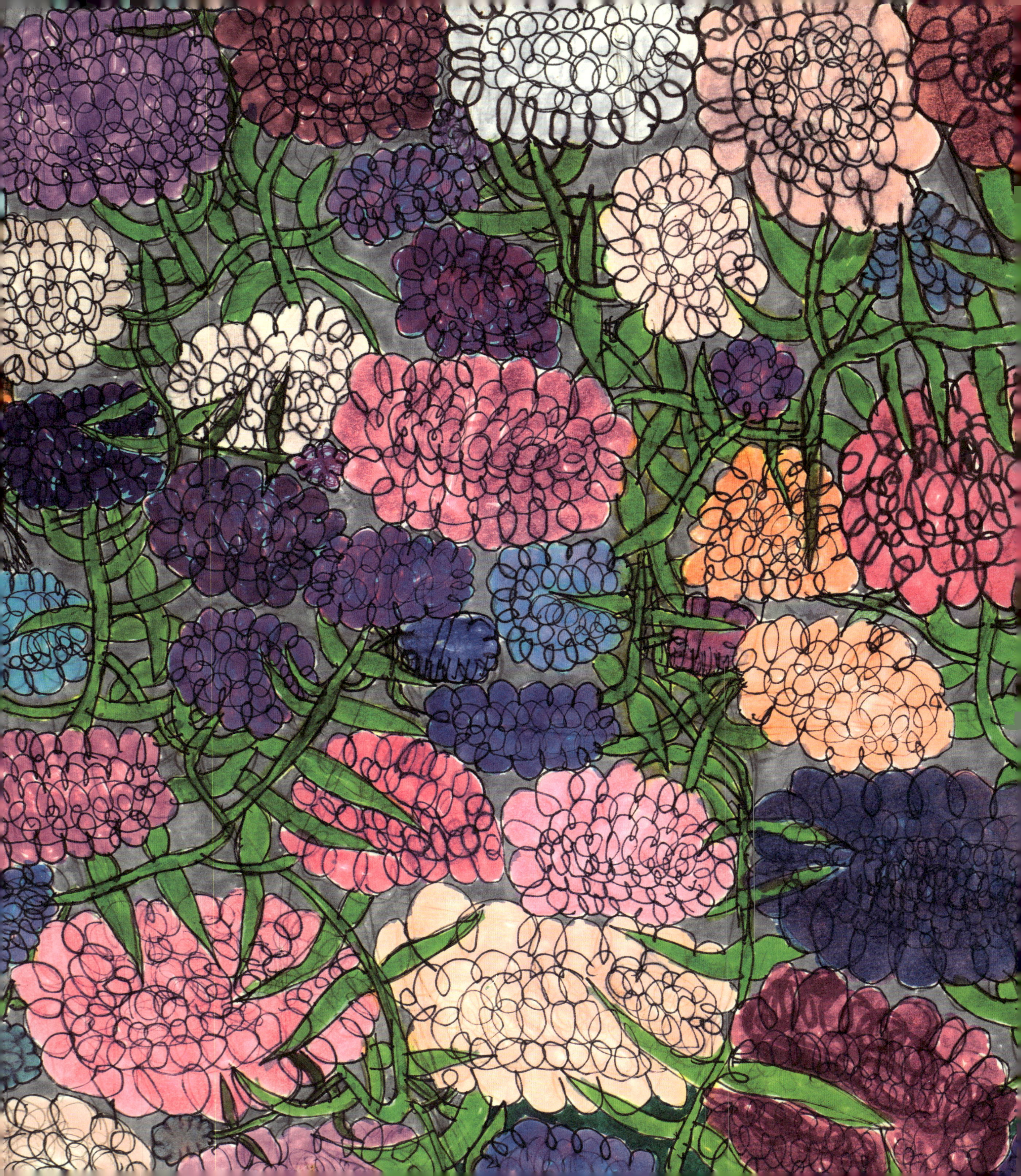